William Jackson Brodribb

Constantinople

Sketch of its History from its Foundation to its Conquest by the Turks in 1453

William Jackson Brodribb

Constantinople

Sketch of its History from its Foundation to its Conquest by the Turks in 1453

ISBN/EAN: 9783743317062

Manufactured in Europe, USA, Canada, Australia, Japa

Cover: Foto ©ninafisch / pixelio.de

Manufactured and distributed by brebook publishing software (www.brebook.com)

William Jackson Brodribb

Constantinople

CONTENTS.

	PAGE
PREFACE	vii
INTRODUCTION	ix

CHAPTER I.
BYZANTIUM—EARLY HISTORY ... 1

CHAPTER II.
BYZANTIUM UNDER THE ROMAN EMPIRE ... 23

CHAPTER III.
CONSTANTINOPLE FROM CONSTANTINE TO JUSTINIAN. A.D. 324–527 ... 42

CHAPTER IV.
CONSTANTINOPLE UNDER JUSTINIAN ... 78

CHAPTER V.
THE ISAURIANS ... 97

CHAPTER VI.
THE MACEDONIANS ... 114

CHAPTER VII.
THE COMNENANS 126

CHAPTER VIII.
THE CITY AND ITS PEOPLE 150

CHAPTER IX.
THE LATIN CONQUEST 158

CHAPTER X.
THE LATIN EMPIRE 186

CHAPTER XI.
THE LAST EMPERORS 212

CHAPTER XII.
FALL OF CONSTANTINOPLE, A.D. 1453 229

PREFACE.

IN this little volume it is intended to present a sketch of the leading events of the history of Constantinople during a period of about 2,000 years. It begins with the slight and meagre accounts which have come down to us of its foundation as Byzantium, and it ends with the conquest of the Turks in 1453, when the Eastern empire finally ceased to exist.

The narrative does not profess to be complete and exhaustive. Nor is it mainly based on original sources. It is, for the most part, a compilation. We have sought to present in a small compass the most striking events of a history which is full of interest. For this purpose we have freely used the great work of Gibbon, Finlay's careful and industrious "History of the Byzantine Empire," and Le Beau's voluminous History of the Lower Empire. But for some portions of the work, the sieges of the city, for example, by Philip and Severus, and the final siege by the Turks, the original sources have been consulted. As a compilation, then, and as an account of a city whose history yields in interest to that of two only, and in dramatic events to that of none, we trust that the work may be found useful and interesting.

There would seem to be no description of the situation and importance of Constantinople so clear, so eloquent, and so minutely accurate, as that of Gibbon. We have therefore transferred it to the following pages, to serve as an introduction, warning our readers that a knowledge of the topography of Constantinople is absolutely necessary to the right understanding of its history. This, which is true of all cities, is more peculiarly true as regards Constantinople. For this reason we have not only preferred to quote Gibbon's account in full, but we have prefixed as frontispiece a map of the city.

INTRODUCTION.

"IF we survey Byzantium in the extent which it acquired with the august name of Constantinople, the figure of the imperial city may be represented under that of an unequal triangle. The obtuse point, which advances towards the east and the shores of Asia, meets and repels the waves of the Thracian Bosporus. The northern side of the city is bounded by the harbour, and the southern is washed by the Propontis, or Sea of Marmora. The basis of the triangle is opposed to the west, and terminates the continent of Europe. But the admirable form and division of the circumjacent land and water cannot, without a more ample explanation, be clearly or sufficiently understood.

"The winding channel through which the waters of the Euxine flow with a rapid and incessant course towards the Mediterranean, received the appellation of Bosporus, a name not less celebrated in the history, than in the fables, of antiquity. A crowd of temples and of votive altars profusely scattered along its steep and woody banks attested the unskilfulness, the terrors, and the devotion of the Grecian navigators, who, after the example of the Argonauts, explored the dangers of the inhospitable Euxine. On these banks tradition long preserved the memory of the palace of Phineus, infested by the obscene harpies; and of the sylvan reign of Amycus, who defied the son of Leda to the combat of the cestus. The straits of the Bosporus are terminated by the Cyanean rocks, which, according to the description of the poets, had once floated on the face of the waters, and were destined by the gods to protect the entrance of the Euxine against the eye of profane curiosity. From the Cyanean rocks to the point and harbour of Byzantium the winding length of the Bosporus extends about sixteen miles, and its most ordinary breadth may be computed at about one mile and a half. The *new* castles of Europe and Asia are constructed, on either continent, upon the foundations of two celebrated temples, of Serapis and of Jupiter Urius. The *old* castles, a work of the Greek emperors, command the narrowest part of the channel, in a place where the opposite banks advance within five hundred paces of each other. These fortresses were destroyed and strengthened by Mahomet the Second, when he meditated the siege of Constantinople; but the Turkish conqueror was most probably ignorant that near two thousand years before his reign Darius had chosen the same situation to connect the two continents by a bridge of boats. At a small distance from the old castles we discover the little town of Chrysopolis, or Scutari, which may almost be considered as the Asiatic suburb of Constantinople. The Bosporus, as it begins to open into the Propontis, passes between Byzantium and Chalcedon. The latter of those cities was built by the Greeks, a few years before the former; and the blindness of its founders, who overlooked the superior advantages of the opposite coast, has been stigmatized by a proverbial expression of contempt.

"The harbour of Constantinople, which may be considered as an arm of the Bosporus, obtained, in a very remote period, the denomination of the *Golden Horn*. The curve which it describes might be compared to the horn of a stag, or as it should seem, with more propriety, to that of an ox. The epithet of *golden* was expressive of the riches which every wind wafted from the most distant countries into the secure and capacious port of Constantinople. The river Lycus, formed by the conflux of two little streams, pours into the harbour a perpetual supply of fresh water, which serves to cleanse the bottom, and to invite the periodical shoals of fish to seek their retreat in that convenient recess. As the vicissitudes of tides are scarcely felt in those seas, the constant depth of the harbour allows goods to be landed on the quays without the assistance of boats; and it has been observed that in many places the largest vessels may rest their prows against the houses, while their sterns are floating in the water. From the mouth of the Lycus to that of the harbour, this arm of the Bosporus is more than seven miles in length. The entrance is about five hundred yards broad, and a strong chain could be occasionally drawn across it, to guard the port and city from the attack of a hostile navy.

"Between the Bosporus and the Hellespont the shores of Europe and Asia, receding on either side, enclose the Sea of Marmora, which was known to the ancients by the denomination of Propontis. The navigation from the issue of the Bosporus to the entrance of the Hellespont is about one hundred and twenty miles. Those who steer their westward course through the middle of the Propontis may at once descry the high lands of Thrace and Bithynia, and never lose sight of the lofty summit of Mount Olympus, covered with eternal snows. They leave on the left a deep gulf, at the bottom of which Nicomedia was seated, the imperial residence of Diocletian; and they pass the small islands of Cyzicus and Proconnesus before they cast anchor at Gallipoli, where the sea, which separates Asia from Europe, is contracted into a narrow channel.

"The geographers who, with the most skilful accuracy, have surveyed the form and extent of the Hellespont, assign about sixty miles for the winding course, and about three miles for the ordinary breadth of those celebrated straits. But the narrowest part of the channel is found to the northward of the old Turkish castles between the cities of Sestus and Abydus. It was here that the adventurous Leander braved the passage of the flood for the possession of his mistress. It was here likewise, in a place where the distance between the opposite banks cannot exceed five hundred paces, that Xerxes imposed a stupendous bridge of boats, for the purpose of transporting into Europe a hundred and seventy myriads of barbarians. A sea contracted within such narrow limits may seem but ill to deserve the singular epithet of *broad*, which Homer, as well as Orpheus, has frequently bestowed on the Hellespont. But our ideas of greatness are of a relative nature. The traveller, and especially the poet, who sailed along the Hellespont, who pursued the windings of the stream, and contemplated the rural scenery which appeared on every side to terminate the prospect, insensibly lost the remembrance of the sea, and his fancy painted those celebrated straits with all the attributes of a mighty river flowing with a swift current in the midst of a woody and inland country, and at length, through a wide mouth, discharging itself into the Ægean or Archipelago. Ancient Troy, seated on an eminence at the foot of Mount Ida, overlooked the mouth of the Hellespont, which scarcely received an accession of waters from the tribute of those immortal rivulets the Simois and the Scamander. The Grecian camp had stretched twelve miles along the shore from the Sigæan to the Rhætean promontory, and the flanks of the army were guarded by the bravest chiefs who fought under the banner of Agamemnon. The first of those promontories was occupied by Achilles with his invincible myrmidons, and the dauntless Ajax pitched his tents on the other. After Ajax had fallen a sacrifice to his disappointed pride and to the ingratitude of the Greeks, his sepulchre was erected on the ground where he had defended the navy against the rage of Jove and of Hector, and the citizens of the rising town of Rhæteum celebrated his memory with divine honours. Before Constantine gave a just preference to the situation of Byzantium, he had conceived the design of erecting the seat of empire on this celebrated spot, from whence the Romans derived their fabulous origin. The extensive plain which lies below ancient Troy, towards the Rhætean promontory and the tomb of Ajax, was first chosen for his new capital; and though the undertaking was soon relinquished, the stately remains of unfinished walls and towers attracted the notice of all who sailed through the straits of the Hellespont.

"We are at present qualified to view the advantageous position of Constantinople, which appears to have been formed by nature for the centre and capital of a great monarchy. Situated in the forty-first degree of latitude, the imperial city commanded, from her seven hills, the opposite shores of Europe and Asia. The climate was healthy and temperate, the soil fertile, the harbour secure and capacious, and the approach on the side of the continent was of small extent and easy defence. The Bosporus and the Hellespont may be considered as the two gates of Constantinople, and the prince who possessed those important passages could always shut them against a naval enemy, and open them to the fleets of commerce. The preservation of the eastern provinces may, in some degree, be ascribed to the policy of Constantine, as the barbarians of the Euxine, who in the preceding age had poured their armaments into the heart of the Mediterranean, soon desisted from the exercise of piracy, and despaired of forcing this insurmountable barrier. When the gates of the Hellespont and Bosporus were shut, the capital still enjoyed within their spacious enclosure every production which could supply the wants or gratify the luxury of its numerous inhabitants. The sea coasts of Thrace and Bithynia, which languish under the weight of Turkish oppression, still exhibit a rich prospect of vineyards, of gardens, and of plentiful harvests; and the Propontis has ever been renowned for an inexhaustible store of the most exquisite fish, that are taken in their stated seasons, without skill, and almost without labour. But when the passages of the straits were thrown open for trade, they alternately admitted the natural and artificial riches of the north and south, of the Euxine and of the Mediterranean. Whatever rude commodities were collected in the forests of Germany and Scythia, and far as the sources of the Tanais and the Borysthenes; whatsoever was manufactured by the skill of Europe or Asia; the corn of Egypt, and the gems and spices of the farthest India—were brought by the varying winds into the port of Constantinople, which, for many ages, attracted the commerce of the ancient world." (Gibbon's *History of the Decline and Fall of the Roman Empire*, chap. xvii.).

CONSTANTINOPLE.

CHAPTER I.

BYZANTIUM.—EARLY HISTORY.

NEW ROME, or the city of Constantine, was known as Byzantium for a period of almost a thousand years. It was a Greek colony, and was in fact one of the most advanced outposts of Greek civilization. The neighbouring region was wild and barbarous. The waters of the Euxine had been the terror of Greek mariners, and were long regarded by them with that vague superstitious awe, out of which is sure to spring a plentiful crop of myth and legend. The sea itself was spoken of as the "Inhospitable,"[1] a name subsequently exchanged for the more pleasing appellation with which we are familiar, and which promises a gracious reception to the stranger who shall venture on its waters. Greek emigrants had found homes along the shores of the Propontis, and from thence would often pass through the famous strait into the greater sea beyond, which now, losing some of its fearfulness and

[1] The "Axine," afterwards "Euxine" (Hospitable).

mystery, would seem worthy of a better and kindlier name. But the old memories still clung to it, and the fleet of the Argonauts, and their perilous passage through the "clashing" or "wandering" islets, as they were called, at the entrance into its waters, and Jason and Medea, and the Golden Fleece, and the weird land of Colchis, must have been present to the mind of every Greek and Roman voyager on the Euxine. A region with more fascinations, both for traveller and historical student, whether in the modern or ancient world, it is difficult to imagine. Whatever interest it may have had in the past, it is assuredly not likely to lose in our own day, and it may in the present generation become the scene of events which, for good or for evil, will immensely affect the destinies of mankind.

It was in the seventh century B.C., probably about 658 B.C., that the city on the Bosporus was originally founded. It was thus younger than Rome by about a century. The Greek genius for colonization was particularly active at this time, and the Thracian Chersonese, or the peninsula of Gallipoli, had already attracted a swarm of settlers, a large proportion of whom had come from Athens. Megara, one of the less politically famous Greek states, but rich and prosperous, was beginning to push out its colonies northwards to the shores of the Propontis, and a site so pre-eminently eligible as that of Byzantium could hardly be overlooked. Chalcedon, on the opposite coast of Bithynia, had already been occupied by emigrants from Megara. But these emigrants had, unluckily for themselves, not shown the usual discernment of Greek colonists; they had, in fact, been so stupid as "to have seen the better, and yet to have chosen the worse." So they were called, by way of jest, the "blind men," the name having, according to Herodotus, been given them by the Persian satrap Megabazus when he was once on a visit to Byzantium, and noted the marvellous advantages of the site. The joke, says the historian, was one of "immortal memory," and the name stuck ever afterwards to the unfortunate citizens of Chalcedon. When the next set of colonists started from Megara for the coasts of Thrace, and asked the oracle of the Pythian Apollo where they should seek their new home, they were directed to a spot opposite the "blind men's" country. On seeing Chalcedon on the Asiatic side of the Bosporus, they at once took the hint, and forthwith crossed to the European shore, and there settled themselves on a site which could not fail to promise a brilliant future for their city.

It is hardly necessary that we should dwell on what has been so repeatedly described, and is now so generally well known, as the singularly convenient situation of Constantinople. It was all that could be desired, both politically and commercially. On the land side the place was easy of defence, and when the new settlers had thrown up some walls and fortifications, they were tolerably safe against the attacks of the barbarous Thracian tribes. Its commercial advantages could hardly be overrated. In quite early days there was a good trade in corn with the countries bordering on the Euxine, and a large revenue could well be raised by the Byzantines out of dues levied on the corn ships. Another great source of wealth was in their fisheries. Huge shoals of fish used to pour down from the Euxine into the Bosporus, and then, for some reason or other, decidedly preferred the European to the Asiatic shore. A multitude of the poorer citizens, so we are told by Aristotle, gained a livelihood as fishermen. Riches, in fact, flowed into the city from all sides, and the deep and splendid harbour to the north was known to Pliny and the ancients, as it is to us, as the Golden Horn, the aptest phrase in the ancient mind for wealth and plenty. The Byzantines, too, had the good luck to have good wine within easy reach, as well as good fish. From Maronea on the Ægean and its neighbourhood came plentiful supplies of a wine so exquisite as to be the talk of the world, and so potent as to give the foreign merchant, after a dinner with his Byzantine friends and customers, little chance of returning sober to his ship. Homer makes Ulysses speak with rapture of its divine bouquet. Byzantium was indeed in all respects a highly favoured city, and life there must have been eminently enjoyable. We fear that they abused their privileges. At any rate, it was whispered that, in later days, they indulged themselves in strange and even shameful irregularities. But this, it seems, was not till democracy had been thoroughly established among them. It is fair to say that one of the writers who speaks unkindly of them was generally reputed to be too harsh and censorious. According to one statement, they came at last wholly to forget the commonest proprieties, and a Byzantine citizen was so immoderately jovial, that he made it a practice himself to live in a public-house, and to let his own residence to some wealthy stranger. Even in the extremity of a siege they could not throw off their careless ways, and the story was told that, in the time of Philip of Macedon, the officers could only keep them to their duty on the ramparts by transferring thither the public-houses and taverns. The very idea of discipline and law seems to have vanished so utterly that one of their mob orators, when he was asked in some case what the law prescribed, was able to reply, "Whatever I please."

Of the history of the city before the fifth century B.C. we know nothing. By that time it is certain that it was prosperous and moderately powerful. Linking, as it did, two continents and their civilizations, being the key of the Ægean and Euxine, and having the singular advantages of which we have spoken, it could not possibly fail to figure in Greek history, and to attract the notice of Persia, as soon as war with Greece had been resolved on. For a long period after its foundation it was quite able to hold its own against its neighbours, and it even appears to have reduced some of them to tributaries. This was its position in the sixth century B.C., at the close of which Dareius Hystaspes made his famous expedition from Asia into Europe. One of his satraps, Otanes, won several considerable conquests on the Propontis and the Bosporus, and among them the cities of Byzantium and Chalcedon. These Greek colonies remained under the power of Persia till that great Ionian revolt, early in the fifth century B.C., which led to the desperate struggle between Greece and Persia, and from which may be said to date Greek fame and grandeur. Byzantium joined the revolt, but its people were soon frightened into submission to the Persians by the approach of a vast Phœnician fleet, and, along with a host of fugitives from their neighbours of Chalcedon, who shared their panic, they sailed away northward into the Euxine, and settled themselves on its western shores at Mesembria, under the extremity of the Haemus range. Their own fair city, with many others in those parts, was burnt to the ground, according to Herodotus, and we hear nothing more about it till the contest between the East and the West was decided by the victory of Plataea, in 479 B.C. The Spartan, Pausanias, who on that memorable day had commanded the Greek army, recovered the place from a Persian garrison for its old inhabitants, and, as he must have wished to restore them something better than a heap of ruins, he came to be spoken of as its founder. The fortunes of the city were now once more identified with those of the Greek world. It was at first its lot to become one of the maritime dependencies of Athens, which, soon after the war with Persia, occupied with colonists the fruitful lands of the Thracian Chersonese, and pushed her fleets through the Hellespont into the Propontis and Euxine. It was to be expected that Byzantium would fall under the control of such a power, and its possession was of course financially very valuable to Athens. Trading vessels from the Euxine would thus be made to swell the Athenian revenue. But when Athens lost both a fleet and an army in the disastrous expedition to Sicily, her loosely compacted empire received a fatal shock, and the revolt of Abydos on the Hellespont in 411 B.C. soon led to the loss of Byzantium and Chalcedon. The star of Sparta was now in the ascendant, and the Byzantines were ready to welcome a Spartan admiral, who was preparing to cut off the Athenian corn supplies from the Euxine. Athens would have been brought to the verge of ruin had he been thoroughly successful, but Sparta was never able to rival her effectually in the headship of allied maritime dependencies. Fortunately, too, she had among her citizens one who was equal to the crisis, and who, at least on this occasion, deserved well of her.

This was the clever and energetic Alcibiades, a man whom we cannot help admiring, though on the whole his career disappoints us. He might, we feel, have done so much more for Athens than he did, and perhaps have even saved her from her great reverse at Syracuse. He now acted promptly. First, he seized Chrysopolis, the modern Scutari, the port of Chalcedon. Shortly afterwards, in 408 B.C., he attempted to win back Chalcedon itself for the Athenians. The place was held by a Spartan garrison, supported by the Persian satrap Pharnabazus. Alcibiades, it seems, had at his disposal a small force of Athenian citizens, and with this he blockaded the place by drawing a wall from the Bosporus to the Propontis. This cut off all communication on the land side, and the Persian satrap was foiled in an attempt to relieve the city, though at the same moment a sortie was led by the Spartan officer within the walls. The end of the matter was that Chalcedon surrendered and again consented to become an Athenian dependency, and to pay both the same tribute for the future as in the past, and to make good to Athens all arrears which had accumulated since the revolt.

Previous to the surrender, Alcibiades began preparations for the more serious and important task of the capture of Byzantium. For this his present resources were not adequate, and he thought it prudent to strengthen himself with an increase of funds and of military force. His first step was to attack Selymbria, on the northern shores of the Propontis, and about fifty miles to the west of Byzantium. It, too, had been a colony from Megara, and it had no doubt passed, along with Byzantium, into the power of Athens. It would have been sure to take part in the revolt of that city from Athens. Alcibiades contrived to secure possession of it by means, it is said, of the treacherous connivance of some of its citizens. Now he was able to get a supply of money, and thus to levy an army from the neighbouring Thracians, always a warlike people, and very formidable when properly led. As soon as the terms of submission had been fixed for Chalcedon, he resolved to attempt the recovery of Byzantium. He advanced on it by land from Selymbria, and began the siege of the city, the first of much importance, in a long series of memorable attacks. The place could be reduced only by regular military operations, and in these, when applied to fortified positions, the Greeks were never very skilful. The siege of a city was certain to be tedious. It was as difficult and hazardous to attempt to carry a strong fortress by assault as it is in these days of breech-loading rifles. Battering engines and the missiles which they hurled could do but little against a resolute and disciplined garrison. On this occasion the defence was under the direction of a Spartan commander, Clearchus, at the head of some Spartan troops, and it seems to have been conducted with a spirit and obstinacy equal to that with which Osman Pasha held his lines at Plevna. All the attacks of the besieging army were successfully repelled, as might have been expected, by Spartan skill and valour. It became evident that the work which the Athenian general had undertaken would be slow and arduous, and that the only mode of accomplishing it would be by means of a close and strict blockade. The Byzantines were cut off from the sea by the enemy's fleet. If they could be closed in on land, their surrender must be only a question of time. So Alcibiades simply converted the siege into a blockade, and waited patiently the pressure of famine which sooner or later would drive the populous city to desperation. As it was, the Byzantines bore their misery till they could bear it no longer. It seems that the Spartan commander did not care much for their sufferings, but coolly saw the unhappy people die in the streets, as long as he could feed his own soldiers. He was a man with all the Spartan hardness and tenacity, and he may have been as much a hero as Leonidas, though, as he failed, he has not won for himself equal glory. He kept the provision stores under lock and key, and persisted in the defence till he felt that if he was to hold Byzantium for Sparta, he must seek succour from without. There was the Persian satrap, Pharnabazus, somewhere in the neighbourhood, and from him he might hope for help. Pharnabazus, he knew, had something of a fleet, and with this it might be possible to menace some of the possessions of Athens, and thereby loosen the grip of the besiegers on Byzantium. After an interval of a few months Clearchus managed to steal out of the city with this view, and impressed on two of his officers that they were to do their best for the defence till aid should arrive. His idea seems to have been that the Byzantines would, with due encouragement, suffer for their own sakes to the last extremity rather than surrender themselves to Athens, from which they could hardly expect very lenient terms. He was, however, deceived. The Byzantines, accustomed no doubt to good living, would not endure further privations. They knew, too, that their neighbours of Chalcedon had after their capitulation secured for themselves a fairly favourable position, and were henceforth to be simply what they had been before, a tributary dependency of Athens. And so perhaps they counted on similar treatment for themselves. Athens, too, it is to be noted, had a repute for kindness and generosity in the Greek world, which Sparta never possessed. We may also take it for granted that there was a party in the city which sincerely regretted the revolt, and was really anxious to have the old connection with the foremost state of Greece restored. The result of all this was that Alcibiades was ultimately successful. There was not, indeed, a regular and unanimous surrender, but some Byzantine citizens—traitors they do not deserve to to be called—admitted the Athenians one night into what was known as the Thracian quarter of the city. The Spartan officers whom Clearchus had entrusted with the defence, remained at their posts, faithful to the orders of their superior, but they were easily overpowered, and were forced into submission. Their lives were spared, and they were sent as prisoners to Athens. Those who had trusted to Athenian clemency were not doomed to disappointment. The Byzantines obtained for themselves the same terms as the citizens of Chalcedon had done. Once more, after a siege of nearly a year, in the winter of 408 B.C., Byzantium returned to its former political condition, and it was one of the most honourable achievements of Alcibiades to have recovered for Athens, as a tributary ally, this most important city.

With the downfall of Athens in 405 B.C., at the fatal battle in the Hellespont, which deprived her of her entire fleet, Byzantium was again for a brief space under Spartan sway, and occupied by a Spartan garrison. But a few years afterwards we find it restored to its old alliance, which on the whole, no doubt, best suited its democratic leanings. We may be tolerably sure that it was a city, the population of which would have been always impatient of the oligarchical government which Sparta favoured. Athens, in fact, was its natural ally, and though soon afterwards, with a somewhat unworthy fickleness, it threw off the alliance and aspired to complete independence, it never became thoroughly hostile in its sentiments to the Athenian people. It is easy to understand that there must always have been a certain sympathy between the two cities, which in many respects resembled each other. Commerce must have done much to draw them together, and to create ties of friendship. There were, doubtless, close intimacies between many Athenian and Byzantine citizens. Still, Byzantium, in the year 356 B.C., joined in a hostile movement against Athens, which caused that state extreme perplexity and serious loss. This was the Social War, as it is called, or the revolt of the allies of Athens. The blow was one from which Athens never really recovered, and which left her too weak to carry on with needful vigour the struggle against Philip of Macedon. Byzantium was thus the means of inflicting a grievous hurt on the one state of Greece which had very soon to fight single-handed for Greek freedom against a semi-barbarous power. This the people of Athens felt very bitterly, though they generously forgave it. It was not long before Byzantium itself was threatened by the formidable king of Macedon, the common enemy of Greece, and was only too glad to receive aid from a quarter whence it had hardly a right to expect it. The city now held an important political position, not unlike, though far less commanding, than that of Athens in past days. It was not only independent, but was also the head of a small confederacy, consisting of the Greek colonies in Thrace and on the shores of the Propontis. Among these were Selymbria and Perinthus, both of which were unsuccessfully attacked by Philip about 340 B.C. The king of Macedon understood how to besiege a city better than any man of his time. The affair was with him a thoroughly scientific operation, and as he had introduced a new system of tactics into warfare generally, so, too, he employed new and more effective machinery in sieges. Selymbria and Perinthus were both important towns; the latter was particularly flourishing, and it is said that it had rivalled, if it had not surpassed, Byzantium, in wealth and population. It was admirably situated for commerce in peace and for defence in war; built, as it was, on a peninsula, with a very narrow neck, down the slope of a steep hill, so as to resemble an amphitheatre. The hill faced landwards, and ended in precipitous cliffs which utterly defied the approach of a fleet. The place, too, was strongly fortified. It would have been a great thing for Philip to have possessed himself of it, and he spared no skill or labour in making the attempt. He attacked it by land and sea, and the siege was a very memorable one. In fact, it marked an epoch in the history of sieges, and it was conducted in a novel fashion and with many new appliances. The citizens made a brave defence, but it would hardly have been successful, had they not been well backed up by their neighbours of Byzantium and the Persian satraps of the adjacent districts, whom the court of Persia, already apprehensive of mischief from the restless ambition of Philip, had directed to help the Greek city to their uttermost. By their means Perinthus was well supplied with stores of all kinds, and with everything which could enable it to confront the peril, and in addition it had the services of an Athenian officer with a body of mercenary troops. Philip battered down the first line of defence, but only to find himself repelled by a far stronger barrier built up out of the houses on the lower part of the slope. Similar barriers might be indefinitely multiplied, and, though Philip was the last man in the world to allow himself to be beaten, he gave up the attempt as hopeless, after a siege of about three months.

His next step was one which it is not easy to understand. Having failed at Perinthus, he marched to Byzantium, and this he did with only a portion of his army, the remainder being left at Perinthus, that he might not seem to own himself altogether foiled. But how could he hope, under the circumstances, to succeed in the capturing such a city as Byzantium? He could do nothing by sea, as the Byzantine fleet was greatly superior to his own. And on the land side the fortifications at this time appear to have been singularly complete. The assailant would have to break through a double wall so formidable that Pausanias speaks of it as one of the strongest he had seen after the famous walls of Messene. Philip must have known that he had a very poor prospect of success, unless there might be a faction within which would favour his designs. A story was told, that after the siege had been raised, he wrote a letter to the Byzantines to the effect that, had he chosen to avail himself of a treacherous offer on the part of one of their distinguished citizens, he might have entered their city. He even mentioned the citizen by name, and the man, it is said, killed himself rather than fall a victim to the popular fury. Philip's statement, if really made by him, was probably a cruel slander. Leon, the citizen to whom he attributed the base intention, seems to have been a man of honour and patriotism. Still we may fairly assume that the sagacious king would never have ventured on so very difficult an enterprise, had he not believed that he saw grounds for hoping something from disunion among the Byzantines. Almost the normal state of a Greek city was one of division and faction. At Byzantium there would be sure to be many who feared and hated Athens, and would be ready to submit to anything rather than again pass under her power. Philip might well think that it might be possible for him to appeal successfully to such persons, and that through them the city might be cajoled into an alliance with himself against Athens. It must have been with some such idea that he made his attempt on Byzantium. But the Byzantines, much to their credit, declined to become his tools, and preferred to stand by the common cause of Greece. The siege they now sustained is an honourable passage in the history of their city.

Great indeed was their peril. Philip, with his powerful and well-trained army, with a fleet too strong to be despised, though no doubt inferior to their own, which almost rivalled that of Athens; above all, with his well-known persistent energy and amazing fertility in resources, was an enemy whom the very strongest city would have good reason to fear. Byzantium was certainly strong and skilfully fortified, but it had wisely and generously given liberal aid to its sister and neighbour Perinthus, and now, as the result, its garrison was not by any means adequate to man its walls on the required scale. It needed trained soldiers to resist such a foe as Philip, and could hardly entrust its defence to volunteer citizens. The average Byzantine had not the moral stamina to take his turn at military duty in the trenches or on the walls. He could not, at a moment's notice, break off the even tenour of his pleasant and luxurious life. While trying to be a soldier, he must be allowed to live in his usual merry, self-indulgent fashion. So if he could not go to his wineshop, he would have his wineshop extemporized for him on the ramparts, or wherever duty might call him. It was, it must be confessed, rather inglorious; and yet through the whole of this terrible crisis these Byzantines acquitted themselves with credit, and really seem to have deserved the succour which at last saved them. The siege lasted about six months. Philip had in his service a particularly clever engineer, Polyidus by name, who was versed in all the then known arts of besieging cities, and who doubtless added many ingenious expedients evolved out of his own wit and genius. New kinds of engines were used, as at Perinthus, and an endless series of underground passages were cut under the walls, to give the assailants a chance of suddenly appearing within the lines of defence. Nor was this all. Across the Golden Horn Philip threw a bridge, and he blocked up the harbour with huge masses of stone, to keep off the approach of the Byzantine ships. On one occasion he was all but successful. It was a dark, wet night, and by means of their subterranean passages the Macedonian troops had contrived to steal within the fortified lines. Luckily, at the right moment, the dogs barked; the Byzantines awoke and were at their posts, and drove back the enemy into his mines. It is said that Heaven specially favoured them, and that a sudden radiance in the form of a crescent streamed across the sky, and showed them all things clearly. The light may have been that of the Aurora Borealis. So striking was the incident that in after times it was thought worthy of being commemorated on the coins of the city, and the crescent represented on them has been supposed (though the idea probably cannot be sustained) to have suggested their famous symbol to the Turks. The Byzantines were as pertinacious in defence as their enemy was in attack, and when his engines shattered their walls and towers, they repaired the breaches with the tombstones from their burial-places. Their ships, too won a decisive victory over his fleet in the Bosporus. Well indeed did they fight, we may say for Greece as well as for themselves, against the might of Macedon.

But it is a question whether they could have successfully prolonged the struggle. There was every reason why the Greeks should come to the rescue of Byzantium, but we know how slow they were to unite even when their common safety seemed imperatively to demand it. On this great occasion the chief islands of the Ægean saw their interest and acted accordingly. A fleet from Rhodes and Cos and Chios was soon in the waters of the Bosporus. Athens, too, though she had little reason to be pleased with the Byzantines, who had deserted her confederacy and contributed mainly to its overthrow, did not forget that she was a Greek city, and ought indeed to be forgiven and saved. So, at the prompting of Demosthenes, she sent ships and soldiers and a good worthy man, the honest upright Phocion, to command them, and the Byzantines received the welcome succour with joy and gratitude. The siege was raised, and the city now, like its sister Perinthus, delivered from the terror of the restless king of Macedon, voted, in full assembly, a decree of honour and a crown of gold of unusual size and splendour to the generous people of Athens.

For some time subsequent to this memorable and successful defence of their city against the power of Macedon we hear but little of the Byzantines. On the occasion of Alexander's expedition into Thrace and his advance to the Danube, they furnished him with a flotilla for operations on that river. We may hence conclude that they had thought it best to become his allies. The city seems to have retained its independence, but it never reduced to subjection any considerable portion of the adjacent regions of Thrace or impressed its Greek civilization on that barbarous country. In fact, it lost ground, and from this time almost down to the Christian era it had to struggle hard for existence against the Thracian tribes, by whom it was harassed with a ceaseless and most troublesome warfare. The citizens could never thoroughly shake off their enemy; no sooner was one attack repelled than another worse and more alarming threatened them. Such is the picture which the historian Polybius gives us of the unhappy lot of the once prosperous Byzantines. They were doomed, he says, to suffer the punishment of Tantalus, as the produce of their rich fields, at the moment they were about to gather it, was swept off under their very eyes by a sudden incursion of barbarians. Still they had the spirit to cling to their old position of a free Greek city. But worse troubles were in store for them. A new peril hung over their city in the third century B.C. The great southward movement of the Gauls, which had well-nigh overwhelmed Rome a century before, now began to threaten Byzantium. Under the leadership of Brennus, a name common, it would seem, among Gallic chieftains, a host of these warlike barbarians had ravaged Macedonia and Thessaly about the year 279 B.C., and even penetrated to Delphi, intent on plundering the sacred treasures of its famous temple. There, however, Greek valour and discipline, though the defenders were but few, as in the days of Leonidas, hurled back the invading multitude and inflicted on them a defeat which a subsequent storm of unusual fury converted into a ruinous disaster. Those who escaped found their way to Thrace, and joined other Gauls who had deserted Brennus and chosen to follow two other chieftains, Leonorius and Lutarius, into that country. They were charmed with the neighbourhood of Byzantium, and after some decisive successes over the Thracian tribes, they settled down in those parts. The Byzantines felt themselves in imminent danger, and sought to avert it by the payment of a large tribute. On this humiliating condition their fruitful lands were to be spared by the invader. But the Gauls could not long hold their conquest. They were beaten and driven out by the native tribes. Byzantium, however, got no relief. The citizens were ground down by payments which had now to be made to their Thracian neighbours. In their distress they begged the Greeks to help them, and, to augment their heavily burdened revenue, they taxed, more rigorously perhaps than ever in the past, every ship which entered the waters of the Euxine.

New complications now arose. All the mercantile world complained bitterly of the loss and inconvenience which Byzantium was inflicting on it. Rhodes was at this time the chief maritime power, and to Rhodes the aggrieved merchants carried their complaints and appealed for redress. First of all, the Rhodians sent an embassy to Byzantium, asking for some remission of the dues. This was refused, and war was then declared against the city about 220 B.C. Rhodes found a useful ally in Prusias, king of Bithynia, to whose court the great Hannibal, some years afterwards, fled as a refugee. Prusias was a powerful prince; he was strong enough to discomfit a host of Gauls which had crossed into Asia on the invitation of Attalus, king of Pergamus, and even to give efficient aid to the Macedonian Philip in his war with Rome. As Prusias was the ally of Rhodes, so was Attalus of the Byzantines. They had hopes, too, of aid from Achaeus, who ruled an extensive dominion in Asia Minor, roughly described by Polybius as the entire country west of the Taurus range. The war began unfavourably for them. Prusias took one of their most important positions, Hieron, which was at the entrance of the Bosporus, and effectually commanded it. This, it seems, they had recently had to purchase at a great cost, which however they thought was profitably incurred. They lost also a strip of territory in Asia, a part of the coast of Mysia, which they had possessed from time immemorial. Achaeus, from whom they had hoped much, disappointed them, and they were now anxious to have the war ended without further loss and disgrace. The result appears to have been attained partly through the intervention of a Gallic king, Cavarus, the ruler of those Gauls who had settled themselves for a time in Thrace, and compelled the Byzantines to pay tribute. Peace was concluded, and Byzantium was to have all that it had lost in the war restored to it, but to levy no dues for the future on ships entering the Euxine.

In Rome's wars in the East during the second and first centuries B.C., it was hardly possible for such a city to remain neutral. Its situation, in fact, precluded it from neutrality. It brought itself into direct connection with Rome by a treaty in the year 148 B.C. At that time Rome was at war with the pseudo-Philip, as he was called, who pretended to be the son of Perseus of Macedon. From that date the city professed to have been an ally of the Romans, as one of the confederate states which retained their liberties. This the Byzantines regarded as an honourable position. Long afterwards,[1] in Nero's reign, they sent envoys to Rome, asking for some remission of tribute on the ground of the services

[1] Tacitus, Annals, xii. 62.

which they had rendered to many Roman generals, to Sulla, Lucullus, and Pompey, among them, in Rome's eastern wars. Cicero, in one of his speeches,[1] was able to speak of Byzantium as specially loyal in its friendship to Rome. One of the heaviest charges he brings against Lucius Piso, the governor of Achaia, was that he had grievously wronged this faithful ally. The city, it seems, was still rich and flourishing, and it was, Cicero adds, known to all the world that it was crowded with statues and works of art. These the Byzantines, though they had had to bear the brunt of the Mithridatic war, had, to their great glory, says the orator, most sedulously and religiously guarded. The city had often indeed been brought low, but it is clear that it had a wonderful capacity of recovering itself. A tributary of Rome, as it had formerly been of Athens, it kept its municipal freedom, and with it not merely material prosperity, but also some sense of dignity and self-respect.

[1] Speech on the Provinces, chap. iv.

CHAPTER II.

BYZANTIUM UNDER THE ROMAN EMPIRE.

UNDER the Emperors of Rome, Byzantium, as far as we know, enjoyed quiet and prosperity. Its citizens, we may assume, were no longer annoyed by their barbarous neighbours, but were, no doubt, able to trade and make money to their hearts' content. For such people the rule of Rome over the world, with the peace and order it established, was a decided advantage. The city must have had many attractions for a rich and cultivated Roman visitor. Its old historical associations were striking, and it was still one of the centres of Greek art and civilization. The student, the antiquarian, the lover of art, and the lover, too, of pleasure and of luxury, would, if circumstances allowed, be sure once in a lifetime to visit such a city. Among those who did so were a very famous Roman couple, whose names are still deservedly familiar to us. These were the great general Germanicus and his noble and high-minded wife Agrippina. Germanicus, in addition to his military ability, was a man of real culture, and he seems to have been keenly eager to explore all the more remarkable parts of the vast Roman empire, those especially in which he might find relics of the religions and civilizations of bygone days. After having fought for Rome in the swamps and forests of Germany, and avenged the slaughtered legions of Varus, he was able to obey an impulse he had long felt, and in the year 18 A.D., the fifth of the reign of Tiberius, he turned his steps eastward, and visited those famous cities, Perinthus and Byzantium. Thence he passed over the strait to the plains of Troy, to see, as Tacitus says,[1] "the birthplace and cradle of the Roman people." It is to be noted that the historian speaks of these two cities as if they were almost included in the Roman province known as Asia, which embraced, of course, only a small portion of what we call Asia Minor. Both cities were under Rome's tutelage, and so, too, was Thrace, or the modern Roumelia. But the country was not as yet actually a province. It was ruled by native kings, the nominees of Rome, as the Herods of Judæa were. Occasionally the country, as might be expected from the turbulent character of the inhabitants, gave trouble; but it was not able to recover its independence. Twice during the reign of Tiberius the Thracian tribes became restive, and dared to defy the power of Rome. They had, it seems, to furnish levies for the Roman armies, and of this they became impatient. Tacitus does not dignify the affair with the name of a war; he calls it merely "a movement." In each case it was soon and easily crushed. The fighting was, it seems, confined to the inland regions,

[1] Annals, ii. 54.

and Byzantium was in no way affected by it. From this date (A.D. 26) we hear nothing about the city or about the country for a considerable time. Claudius, according to one account, made it from a dependency into a province; but Suetonius, the biographer of the twelve Cæsars, says[1] that this was done in Vespasian's reign from 70 A.D. to 79. He mentions both Byzantium and Thrace as having then been formally constituted into provinces. The city, we should suppose, could not itself have been a separate province; it was probably included either in Thrace or in Asia. Its general condition would remain practically unchanged, and it no doubt continued to enjoy many special privileges.

We now lose sight of Byzantium for a long period. Not till the close of the second century does it again appear in history. The empire was then distracted by civil war. The emperor was himself usually a creature of the soldiery. In 193 A.D., Didius Julianus purchased the rule of the Roman world, by offering to the soldiers of the prætorian guard a higher bounty than his competitor. The wretched man was deserted by them in a few days, and executed by the senate's order. By a decree of the same body, Septimus Severus was called to the empire. The choice, on the whole, was a good one; Severus had shown ability as the governor of one of the divisions of Gaul, and he now held a foremost position, being commander of the legions in Illyria and Pannonia. The army at once accepted him as an emperor. On reaching Rome he made the prætorian

[1] Life of Vespasian, chap. viii.

soldiers know that he was their master, and by the terror of some of his own picked troops he drove them to a distance of a hundred miles from the city. His character is a singular study. With much practical good sense and skill in administration was blended a strong vein of superstition, and he is said to have taken a profound interest in magic and astrology. His wife, Julia Domna, whom he had married from Syria, was a very remarkable lady, superstitious, clever, and literary. She was, though this may be scandal, morally weak, and it is very possible that her alleged leaning towards Christianity may have been nothing better than a fondness for Eastern ceremonies and rituals. It seems that she had considerable influence over her husband. Severus, it is said, looked rather kindly on Christianity. The truth is, that by this time the Christian Church was a powerful force in the world, and could not be ignored, though it was not ripe for distinct political recognition. In the eastern half of the empire it had undoubtedly produced effects which had all the promise of permanence. This, with other influences, tended to that separation of the Eastern from the Western world, which was ultimately accomplished. The time seemed to be approaching when the former would wish to be independent of Rome, and would claim a centre of its own.

Severus, then, had been proclaimed emperor, but he had formidable rivals. Albinus in Gaul and Niger in Syria were at the head of armies which were prepared to support them. Over both Severus was decisively victorious. It is only his war with Niger which concerns us. Gibbon has noted an important difference between the civil wars of this period and those of modern Europe. The last have been long and protracted, fought out with all the obstinacy which naturally accompanies the vindication of some great and important principle. The cause of religion or of freedom has been usually involved in them. Not so with these wars of the Roman empire. They were fought not between nations and peoples, but merely between generals and soldiers. As Gibbon says, "The Romans, after the fall of the republic, combated only for the choice of masters." In such struggles, the provinces, and mankind generally, were but uninterested spectators, and cared very little for the result. Hence these wars, unlike those of modern days, were very brief, and one or two battles decided them. The successes of Severus were rapid and complete. Having crossed the Hellespont into Asia with part of his army, he utterly defeated Niger near Issus, where more than five centuries before Alexander had won his second great victory over Dareius. But his work was not yet done. Niger was a man who inspired respect and might be thought worthy of empire. There were those who still clung to him. One city was faithful to his cause, and put forth all its powers of resistance. It was Byzantium. The city may have felt that it had a right to become the head of an Eastern empire.

It seems that the Byzantines may not unreasonably have been confident in their ability to sustain a siege. Their fortifications were the admiration of the world, and their strong and lofty walls, we are told, were so skilfully built and cemented that they presented the appearance of one vast continuous block of stone. Visitors to the city in after days hardly knew whether to wonder most at the art and finish displayed in their origin and construction, or at the destructive power of the besieging army of Severus. The Byzantines, too, were well furnished with every appliance which science could contrive for the purposes of defence. They had engines, it is said, which could lift ships out of the water; and, what was far better, they had an engineer officer of the first capacity to organise the defence. The man's name was Priscus, and so much did he impress Severus by his singular skill and tenacity, that the emperor subsequently took him into his service and availed himself of his talents. The city had also a numerous and well-appointed fleet. Three hundred vessels of every variety, well piloted and manned, some armed with particularly formidable beaks, were at the disposal of the Byzantines.

For the unusually long period of three years they defended themselves; and their brave persistency amid the sufferings which so prolonged a struggle necessarily involved, shows plainly enough that in great emergencies these citizens, who had the character of being mere lovers of ease and comfort, could rise to a high degree of patriotism and loyalty. Severus, it seems, though he did not personally conduct the siege, had staked everything on success, and be the cost what it might, he must capture Byzantium to secure his power in the East. He had one decided advantage. Already by his victories over Niger he had made himself completely master of the resources of all the neighbouring districts, and was thus able to keep his army well supplied. If, therefore, he could beat the Byzantines on the sea, he was sure of final success. He must, however, have had to pay dearly for it. Of his ships, he lost a great number by the sudden and skilful attacks of the besieged, whose practised divers contrived to attach ropes to them under water, and to haul them in as prizes to the city's harbour. When their own vessels needed repair, they did not spare the timbers of their houses, and even the ladies willingly parted with their hair, as those of Carthage are said to have done, for the manufacture of cables. When their walls were threatened with assault, they drove back the enemy with stones dragged out of the public buildings, and even hurled on them statues of bronze, whole and entire. It must indeed have been a bad time for those treasures of art in which Byzantium was so rich. The citizens had clearly made up their minds to spare neither themselves nor their most precious possessions, but to fight on to the dreadful end. It was some time before they were distressed by scarcity. At last they were reduced to chewing leathern hides soaked in water, and finally, it is said, to the dire and horrible extremity in which the weak become literally the prey of the strong. Some attempted an escape from these horrors, and taking advantage of a violent storm, ventured into their boats, resolved to perish or to get supplies of food. But the enemy pounced with his galleys on the unhappy vessels, which were dangerously overcrowded, and, instead of anything like an engagement, there was a mere work of destruction and massacre. The poor creatures were slain or drowned to a man. The dreadful sight was witnessed from the city, and all that day and all the following night were heard piercing cries of grief from the citizens, every one of whom had doubtless seen with his own eyes the miserable death of kinsfolk and friends. Bloodstained fragments of the wrecked vessels were carried to the shores of Asia, and testified to the calamity and to the approaching fall of Byzantium, before the news had been conveyed by word of mouth. On the day after, the waters of the harbour were literally strewn with corpses, which were every moment washed on the beach, forcing on the Byzantines a yet more vivid realization, if possible, of the awful catastrophe. It was now high time for them to surrender. The remainder of the citizens were spared, but the soldiers and the magistrates were put to death. "So we have taken Byzantium," said Severus, who was with his army in Mesopotamia. He was not a generous conqueror on this occasion. He deprived the city of its municipal liberties and its political position, confiscated the property of its citizens, giving all this, along with its adjacent territory, to the people of its old neighbour, Perinthus. These, it appears, showed little pity for their friends and allies of past days, but treated them as despicable villagers, and put on them every sort of indignity. But what most grieved the Byzantines was the destruction of their noble walls, which had long been their pride and glory. Severus had them demolished as far as was possible with such a substantial structure. Thereby he destroyed one of

Rome's great safeguards against the barbarian tribes of Asia and Pontus. Against these Byzantium was both a defence and a place of refuge. This fact is noted by the historian[1] who has described the siege and fall of the city, and it seems to have much impressed him. "I have seen," he says, "those walls in their ruined state, captured and destroyed, one would have thought, by others than Romans; and I had gazed on them when they were still standing." It was a cruel and disastrous work which the besiegers had wrought on the fair city.

After an interval of about a century, we again come to a period which Gibbon describes as one of civil war and confusion. Diocletian's well-meant attempt to organize the administration of an empire, which new forces beyond all human control were more and more tending to dissolve, ended, at the beginning of the fourth century, in the simultaneous rule, or rather misrule, of six emperors. The Goths meanwhile had been menacing the Roman frontiers, and the Euxine, the Bosporus, and the Ægean had felt the presence of their multitudinous war-ships. The Emperor Decius with his whole army had perished by their hands somewhere near the Balkan range in 251 A.D. Soon afterwards they plundered some of the chief cities in the north-west of Asia Minor, and even sacked Chalcedon. The Byzantines must have trembled, although by this time their fortifications may well have been strongly rebuilt. For awhile the barbarians, after having threatened Byzantium and advanced

---

[1] Dion Cassius, in this part of his work unfortunately represented by his epitomiser, Xiphilinus.

as far as Thessalonica, were decisively checked by the Emperor Claudius II., who earned the surname of Gothicus by well-nigh destroying the whole invading host at Nissa on the borders of Servia and Bulgaria, the birthplace probably of the Emperor Constantine. Within, however, three years of this great triumph, which was won in 269 B.C., and achieved, it seems, with Byzantine aid, we find that Claudius's successor, Aurelian, was glad to give up Dacia to the Goths altogether, and to curtail the empire in this direction within the boundary of the Danube. They appear to have been unusually quiet for some years, till they saw their advantage in the troublous period between Diocletian's death and Constantine's final establishment in 324 A.D. as the sole ruler of the world. They crossed the Danube, their lately assigned limit, into Illyricum; but Constantine, who had himself the charge of the province, drove them back beyond the river, and made them sue humbly for peace. One condition, it is said, was that they should furnish the Roman armies with troops to the number of 40,000. Dacia, too, and much more territory, according to Eusebius, was wrested from them, but Eusebius, we must remember, is a persistent panegyrist of Constantine. Not much, probably, that could be called effectual re-conquest, was really accomplished by his arms.

The miserable period of civil strife may be said to have lasted sixteen years, from 308 B.C. to 324 B.C. Constantine's ultimate success may be fairly described as providential, and it was perhaps deserved. One of his rivals, Maxentius, his victory over whom in 312 is commemorated in the tasteless sculpture of the arch of Constantine, was by all accounts a brutal and licentious man, utterly unworthy of empire. The other, also his brother-in-law, Licinius, by birth a Dacian peasant, was indeed an able soldier, but had all the cruelty and treachery of an Eastern despot. The struggle between them was not decided by a single battle, or indeed very speedily. After the fall of Maxentius, the world was divided between the two, Constantine being supreme in the west, Licinius in the east. Both had great fleets and armies, and the war was on a scale equal to that which had ended more than three centuries before in the victory of Augustus at Actium. It was really decided, though not at once terminated, by a battle at Adrianople in 323 B.C. Licinius was driven out of a fortified position, and his army was routed with frightful slaughter. He fell back on Byzantium, the siege of which it was now necessary for Constantine to undertake.

The defences of the city had, it appears, been thoroughly restored, and were strong enough to keep an assailant at bay. But the chief difficulty of the besieging army at first was in supplying themselves with provisions. The city was perfectly safe from any such danger as long as Licinius commanded the Hellespont with his fleet. It was not easy to see how his ships were to be driven from the narrow strait, but it was evident that the attempt must be made if the siege was to be brought to a successful issue. To carry the place by a sudden assault on the land side, in the face of a numerous garrison, was, it may be assumed, beyond

Constantine's power. All that he could do was to wait patiently till his engines had battered down a considerable portion of the fortifications, and meanwhile his soldiers would starve, unless he could get command of the sea. So the officers of his fleet had peremptory orders to force the passage of the Hellespont. At this crisis his eldest son Crispus, whose death twenty years after on a charge of treason has usually been considered one of the blackest stains on Constantine's memory, won a great name for himself, and ensured his father's ultimate triumph. After a few days' hard fighting, he at last dislodged the enemy, and drove him, with the loss of a number of his vessels, from the Hellespont into the Propontis, and thence to the Asiatic shore. There the admiral of Licinius found refuge for a while at Chalcedon.

Constantine's army was now relieved from all danger of famine. It was able to prosecute the siege vigorously, and this it seems to have done with every sort of appliance then known to military art. The science of besieging had made but little, if any, progress since the first century, and Byzantium was probably assailed on this occasion by the same methods and with engines of the same construction as had been employed by Titus in the siege of Jerusalem. Earthworks were thrown up equal in height to the city walls, and on these were planted towers, from which stones and other missiles were hurled on the garrison. Licinius does not seem to have shown any remarkable tenacity in the defence. The city surrendered in the same year, and he himself crossed over to Chalcedon, whither, as we have seen, the admiral of his fleet had fled a short time before.

Thus the famous city, almost ten centuries after its foundation, fell into the hands of Constantine, who was now sole emperor of the Roman world. His success was soon rendered complete by the defeat of Licinius at Scutari, who, with a hastily levied army, attempted a feeble resistance. The conqueror promised to spare his life after his surrender, which was abject and contemptible, and quite unworthy of one who had aspired to empire. But neither did Constantine show much nobleness of character. It is to be feared, though history is rather obscure, that he broke his promise, and, without any adequate justification, had his late rival put to death at Thessalonica, whither he had been permitted to retire. Of course there was a story that he had planned a conspiracy. Licinius, perhaps, hardly deserves our pity, but when we remember that he was the husband of Constantine's sister, and that she had pleaded for his life, we feel that his end, though unhappily by no means without precedent, is something of a blot on the fame of the first Christian emperor.

A great revolution which was to have enduring effects had been accomplished. The fragments of the empire were again united under one head; the seat of government was to be transferred from the city on the Tiber to that on the Bosporus, and Christianity was to be the established religion, we may say, of the world. As always happens, there had been a long, gradual preparation for the change, but still it is no wonder that the man by whom it was directly consummated should have been styled "the Great." Yet we almost grudge Constantine the epithet. He was undoubtedly a good soldier and able administrator, and he must have had patience and energy, both praiseworthy qualities. He had some enlightened ideas of legislation, and seems on the whole to have aimed at the general good of mankind, as far as he understood it. He may, too, have been far-seeing, though we question whether he had quite enough depth and solidity of character to be so. Gibbon's estimate of him is not particularly flattering, and for this there may have been special and obvious reasons; but we do not think that it is singularly unfair. He is, in short, one of those men whom, though they have accomplished great and even worthy things, it is barely possible to admire. His wars with Maxentius and Licinius may be favourably regarded, and their result was satisfactory, inasmuch as they saved the world from rulers infinitely worse than himself. But there are passages in his history which suggest that he was really capable of cold-blooded cruelty, and was not, like Alexander, the mere victim of an occasional violent and savage impulse. He was, it seems, of a calculating turn of mind, without much generosity, and by no means always swayed by very high motives. It would, however, be grossly unjust to brand him as a thoroughly selfish man and a conscious hypocrite. With much worldly sagacity he combined, like Severus, strange superstitious sentiments, which to us are indeed perplexing, and are yet not absolutely unintelligible, when we call to mind some of the grotesque vagaries of our own enlightened age. There may very possibly have been better feelings in him which inclined him towards Christianity, and we can quite believe that he thought he was putting himself on what was deservedly the winning side. But how far his Christianity was thoroughly genuine it is hard to say. He may have thought that it was on the whole good for the world, and that the time was ripe for a change, but he had scarcely strong enough convictions, we should suppose, to make him feel the immense moral worth and permanent value of the new religion. He has, perhaps, been sometimes judged by too high a standard because he professed Christianity and presided at the general Council of Nice. In many of his notions it is certain that he was thoroughly pagan, though he did what he could outwardly to discourage paganism. To call him a saint looks almost like a wilful untruth. To call him "great" makes us prefer to think of what he did rather than of what he was. The year 324 B.C., however, in which Byzantium became the seat of empire, and was henceforth to be known as the city of Constantine, was assuredly a great epoch in the world's history.

If Constantine cannot be strictly said to have founded a new city, he at least established a new capital, and inaugurated a new order of things, which in many of its features was to last for more than eleven centuries. He wished to be regarded by posterity as its founder, and in obedience to ancient custom he went through a solemn ceremonial, in which paganism and Christianity were strangely blended. In his hands he is said to have carried a golden image of the Fortune of the city—a distinct relic this of the old Roman religion—in which such a divinity was acknowledged. He was asked by some of his attendants—as moving at the head of a long procession he was marking out boundaries which seemed to denote a city of unusual dimensions—where he meant to halt, and replied, "When He who goes before me thinks fit to stop." "The incident," Gibbon remarks, "is characteristic and probably true." The city, indeed, was greatly enlarged, though not carried to its future extent, and embracing Galata or Pera. It was still confined to the region south of its harbour. New fortifications, however, were substituted for the old, and these, though not at the time completed, were designed to enclose five out of seven hills of the city. The work was well executed, as is plainly attested by existing remains, which can be traced along about four miles from the harbour to the Sea of Marmora. It was natural that Constantine should wish New Rome to be in most respects a copy of the old city. There must be a forum and a circus, and porticoes, baths, and aqueducts. Although Constantine built several Christian churches, the city must have had a thoroughly pagan aspect, as it was richly adorned with the statues of gods and goddesses from all parts of Greece and Asia. It could be said by Jerome that the dedication of Constantinople involved the stripping bare of almost every city in the world. Still, all the efforts of Constantine failed to make his city equal to Rome in size, population, and grandeur.

There are in truth limits to what the most enterprising man can accomplish; and from the beginning Constantine's work had in it many elements of weakness, which could not be avoided. The city, as he made it, was an artificial product; it did not grow slowly into greatness, as Rome had done. It thus laboured under a serious disadvantage, which affected it for evil throughout its whole history. In many respects it was a bad copy of the old city. Several of the most vicious features of Rome were reproduced in Constantinople. It was comparatively easy for Constantine to attract new citizens; any city, indeed, which is made a seat of government must become moderately populous, and even already the new capital must have been well furnished with inhabitants. We hear of the desertion of Rome by its old and noble families, which are said to have followed the emperor to the Bosporus. But these stories are mainly due to the lively Greek imagination. Rome was not quite shorn of its glory or of its population. We may assume that a number of rich idlers gladly accepted Constantine's invitation to settle in his city. Some he bribed to live there, giving them estates in the neighbouring districts of Asia Minor on condition that they were to maintain a town establishment. These people, we may be sure, had no sort of patriotism or good principle. The poor and lower class were kept, as at Rome, by what was called the emperor's bounty; that is, they lived in perpetual idleness on supplies of corn furnished by the farmers of Egypt, whose industry was thus taxed for the benefit of a demoralized populace. We can hardly wonder that Constantine should have transported this wretched practice, this *panem et circenses* indulgence, to his favourite city, and perhaps we cannot censure him very severely for doing so. He was only following an imperial tradition, and it would be too much to expect that he should have foreseen its pernicious and degrading consequences. Unhappily, the city population became in great part a set of mere pleasure-loving loungers, without serious thought, without sense of duty, or much care for the future. This, indeed, was a bad beginning. Gibbon notes one significant fact, which marks with fatal clearness the utter decay of all manly qualities. So unable were the emperor's degenerate subjects to endure the military profession, that they would cut off the fingers of their right hand rather than be pressed into the service of their country. The empire had to fight its battles with Goths and Germans—good soldiers indeed, but as dangerous for the Romans wholly to rely on as the Sepoys would be to us. Almost everything, under such circumstances, depended on the emperor's personal character, and if he were weak or vicious, the entire fabric of which he was the head was in imminent jeopardy. At the same time, the greatest of men could do nothing more than arrest for a time the decline of the Roman world.

There was thus but little promise of a really noble future for the Eastern empire. Its first beginnings were fraught with evil, and it must have soon perished ingloriously, had it not still retained some of those lessons of order and of freedom which Rome had taught the world.

But for this it would have sunk into a mere oriental despotism, which, indeed, it often dangerously resembled. Its Christianity, too, though not of the best and highest type, must have been a source of strength to it, and have been the means of raising up a number of men whose influence for good would be widely and powerfully felt. For however much the Christian religion may by human error and perverseness become corrupted, it can never wholly lose its great moral worth, or altogether fail to ally itself with some of our better feelings and instincts. The Christianity, indeed, of the East was far too metaphysical and too much addicted to subtle discussion of dogmas; but it had, we know, some truly noble representatives, and we may well believe that there were many whom it rescued from a low and unworthy life. But it was not such a power on the side of virtue and true progress as it ultimately became in the West. To this, among other causes, we may ascribe much of the feeble and unprogressive character of the Byzantine empire, and the consequent dulness of a great portion of its history.

CHAPTER III.

CONSTANTINOPLE FROM CONSTANTINE TO JUSTINIAN.
A.D. 324-527.

WITH a new capital and a new religion, Constantine may perhaps have flattered himself that he had settled everything on a perfectly satisfactory basis. He certainly had reasons for believing that his city was in all respects well fitted to be the seat of the world's government, and that now at length the Christian Church bid fair to win supremacy over men's minds and consciences. His leading thought, no doubt, was to secure the empire against anarchy and civil strife, and this was to be accomplished by uniting the forces of Roman Imperialism and of the Church. But he saw that he could not do this at Rome, which, with Italy, was still too much under pagan influence, whereas in the East the new faith was already in the ascendant among all classes, and was every day becoming more powerful. Probably the empire was too vast, and made up of provinces too unlike in character, and communication between its different portions was too slow and difficult, to allow it to be effectively directed by one head. But Constantine—indeed, any statesman of the time—would naturally suppose that this was the only solution of the difficulty, and that to avert anarchy there must be a strong central administration. This it was which he did his best to create, and he did his work with much ability; but one of the inevitable results was a want of sympathy between the government and the governed. The administration was in the hands of a multitude of imperial officials: it was a bureaucracy, with all the weaknesses of that system. How Constantine could have done otherwise in the interests of order, it is not easy to see. The empire had to be held together, and there was apparently only one way of preserving its unity; but unfortunately that way was one which led to a method of government in which anything like national feeling and a sense of responsibility among the governed had no place. At the same time, some of Constantine's reforms were really wise and beneficial, and as they were on a great scale, and produced lasting effects, we may fairly call him a great legislator. Henceforth the emperor was not, as he had been, so much a military commander-in-chief as a political ruler, and the army was thus subordinated to the civil power. Justice, too, was more regularly administered, and, with better laws, oppression was rendered less easy. To this result Christianity largely contributed. Cruel punishments—that of crucifixion among them—were abolished; the rigours of imprisonment were softened; slavery itself was fenced by restrictions tending to make it tolerable. The Jew, the heathen, could not have a Christian slave, and many ways were opened to the attainment of freedom. Parents were no longer allowed to expose or to sell their children. If they could not support them, provision was made for them at the public cost, after the manner of our parochial relief. Constantine's legislation, on the whole, certainly conduced to the morality and happiness of his subjects. With the Church and clergy he dealt liberally: he gave them privileges, a good social position, and handsome endowments; the public purse was always open to them, and they were put in the way to grow rich and influential. But he kept them under a tight rein, and was quite as much the head of the Church as he was of the State. As such, he summoned the first general council, the famous Council of Nice, in 325, which condemned the theology of Arius.

In one important respect his government was felt to be oppressive. It was very costly, and taxation in those days was carried out in a clumsy fashion, and on what we regard as thoroughly bad principles. A system of administration which attempted so much as that of Constantine could not possibly dispense with an immense revenue, and this was raised by methods which really discouraged industry and economy. Everything seemed to be sacrificed to the imperial court and its belongings, the property of the clergy alone being somewhat favoured. The emperor's palace in its establishment was made a very heavy, and to a great extent a useless, burden on the resources of the empire. Constantine's idea was, no doubt, partly to have a number of well-paid offices which might attract men of ability, partly to impress the people with the spectacle of outward magnificence. But for all this the cultivator of the soil had to pay heavily in the shape of a land-tax; and though the greed of tax-gatherers was restrained by a number of laws devised by Constantine for the protection of his subjects, the fact remained that a useful class of the community was grievously oppressed for the benefit and enrichment of the emperor's household. Matters were made worse by legislative attempts to bind a man down to the condition in which he happened to be born. The son of a farmer or landed proprietor was obliged to abide in his father's calling, unless he had a brother to take his place and to pay the land-tax. In fact, the rural population was tied to the soil, and reduced to serfdom. These people, which had been the strength of Rome's armies, had now to be disarmed, lest they should rise in rebellion. They could not become soldiers, and thus the soldier-class became a distinct one, quite apart from the rest of the community. The military profession almost became hereditary. The result was that emperor and army and the whole machinery of government were out of sympathy with the people. But the system had some compensating advantages. Of patriotic and political virtue there could be but little in a state of things in which the people had no voice and could express no opinion about public affairs; but there is reason to believe that the lower orders had an easier and more comfortable existence than in the periods which we associate with the greatest glories of Greece and of Rome.

This is not the place to tell the story of the fortunes of Constantine's three unhappy sons, between whom, contrary to what we might have expected, he divided his empire. Not one of them was at all fit to reign, and Constantius, a cruel and weak man, after a very brief tenure of empire, made way by his opportune death for Julian, who, if he was a pedant and a fanatic, had some real merits. Julian was sole emperor from 361 to 363. His expedition against Persia, then ruled by the warlike and formidable Sapor, was a failure, and cost him his life. Its conclusion was peculiarly inglorious, as Julian's successor, Jovian, had to make peace with the enemy by ceding to him the five provinces east of the Tigris, with the very important city Nisibis, the fortifications of which were the chief bulwark of the Roman empire in those remote regions. This was, indeed, an epoch in Rome's decline, which we may compare with the abandonment of Britain in the following century. It was a confession of weakness. A brave soldier, a native of Illyria, who had fought with glory under Julian in Persia, was now chosen emperor by the imperial ministers in preference to several candidates. This was Valentinian. As was natural, he was the favourite of the army. He was probably nothing more than a brave and capable officer, and may have at once felt that if he was to hold empire he must divide the responsibility. The late disastrous war with Persia may have led him to this decision; perhaps, too, being a plain soldier without much education, he may have thought he was peculiarly ill-fitted to reign over the more highly polished eastern half of the Roman world. "The weight of the universe," he is represented as saying, "is too great for the hands of a feeble mortal." So he associated with him as his colleague in empire his brother Valens, who was indeed grateful for the honour conferred on him, but who seems to have had no great and worthy qualities. The choice, in fact, as the event proved, was altogether an unfortunate one, and ended in a deplorable calamity. Hitherto the theory had been that the empire should have a single head. Now at last, in the year 364, it was finally and once for all divided, the division being formally executed by the two brothers near Nissa, a name which we have before had occasion to mention. Valentinian was to be the emperor of the West, Valens of the East, and on this understanding they took leave of each other. And now a result, for which circumstances had long been preparing the way and which on the whole could not be regretted, was thus at last accomplished.

Valens is for two reasons a well-known name. To the readers of ecclesiastical history he is the furious Arian and savage persecutor of the orthodox or Athanasian party. To those who follow with interest the declining fortunes of Rome's empire, he figures as one of the most unfortunate of her rulers, perishing as he did in as fatal a reverse as ever befell the Roman arms. It was in the reign of Valens, from 364 to 378, that the Huns first appeared in Europe, and drove before them the Goths, then in some degree a civilized and Christian people, to the banks of the Danube. We must bear in mind that for some time past the Goths had been on peaceful and even friendly terms with the empire, and had supplied a great number of its soldiers. Now in their distress they sought its protection, and prayed that they might be allowed to cross the Danube and to settle in Thrace, as Roman subjects. Their prayer was granted, and they were to be received into Roman territory on condition of surrendering their arms, giving up their children as hostages for their good behaviour, and letting them be dispersed throughout the province of Asia. All this, in their dismay at the Huns, they conceded, and after some delay, and with much difficulty and danger and loss, one of the three great tribes of the Gothic people, the Visigoths, were conveyed across the broad and rapid stream of the Danube. But by a fatal error, due, it would seem, to the covetousness and dishonesty of the emperor's ministers, who let themselves be bribed into disregarding the most important of the conditions required from the Goths, the vast multitude were permitted to retain their arms, and now they stood, a formidable and threatening host, on the plains of Bulgaria. It seems that many of them were very rich, and this stimulated the greedy Romans to charge them extortionate prices for the necessaries of life. The Goths bore it patiently for a time, thinking, perhaps, that it was better to be robbed in peace and safety than to fall a prey to the terrible Huns. But at last they were provoked beyond endurance, and somewhere near Shumla, their leader, Fritigern, who had their entire confidence, roused them to action against their mean and grasping oppressors. The Roman officer on the spot, Lupicinus, who, to quote Gibbon's words, "had dared to provoke, who had neglected to destroy, and who had presumed to despise them," could not withstand their might, and his legions were broken and put to flight by their resolute onslaught. "That day," says the Gothic historian Jornandes, "put an end to the distress of the barbarians and the security of the Romans." The regions south of the Danube, all Moesia and Thrace, were now open to the Goths, and were not spared by them. These fruitful provinces were cruelly ravaged, and though they could not capture the cities, yet soon, to the terror and dismay of the Romans, the Gothic host, to the number of 200,000 men, were under the walls of Adrianople.

Valens at this perilous crisis was at Antioch. Persia was still under the formidable Sapor, and it was necessary to watch his movements and to guard the frontier. Valens, who does not seem generally to have been a man of any conspicuous energy and ability, was prompt on this occasion, and withdrew the legions from Armenia for the defence of his capital and its neighbourhood. He asked aid from his nephew, Gratian, now the emperor of the West. Gratian, who was but nineteen years of age, had just won a decisive victory in Alsace over the Alemanni, a powerful confederation of German tribes, and he was quite prepared and willing to throw the whole weight of his power into the approaching conflict with the Goths. Valens ought to have waited for his arrival, and then he might have confidently reckoned on success. As it was, as soon as he reached Constantinople, he was pressed by the ignorant and clamorous populace to lead his army instantly against the barbarians who had dared to intrude themselves into Roman territory. One is not surprised to hear that these silly, bragging townspeople, who cared for nothing but the amusements of the circus, assured him that if only arms were put into their hands, they would drive the Goths back to their settlements on the other side of the Danube. Provoked by all this popular clamour, and possibly, too, by some jealousy of Gratian, Valens took the rash resolution of at once encountering the enemy. He advanced on Adrianople, and encamped near the city, strengthening his position in the usual Roman fashion with a fosse and rampart. Even now, had he listened to the prudent counsels of one of his generals, all would have been well. Gratian was advancing by rapid marches, and the two armies, it may be presumed, would have overpowered the Goths. But Valens was eager to snatch a victory, and on the ninth day of August, in the year 378 A.D., as black a day in the Roman calendar as that of Allia or Cannæ, he marched to attack the enemy, who was now about twelve miles from the city. His troops, weary and exhausted by exposure for several hours to a burning sun, must have been unfit for battle; and though they seem to have fought bravely, they must have fought at a great disadvantage. The cavalry of the Goths, numerous and well mounted, cooped them into narrow limits, within which the Roman legionaries could not use with effect their formidable javelins or manœuvre in their accustomed manner. The battle seems somewhat to have resembled that of Cannæ, and its end was far more disastrous. Valens and his staff perished in a cottage in which they had taken refuge and which the enemy fired. Two-thirds of his army were slain. The Goths were now in undisturbed possession of the entire country south of the Danube.

It was fortunate for the empire that it contained several strongly fortified cities. This indeed was its preservation. In this respect the East was better able to resist the tide of barbaric invasion than the West. The Goths were brave warriors and even good soldiers, but they had no idea of conducting a siege, and their fierce assault on Adrianople was repelled by the skill and resolution of the defenders. They could not face the volleys of missiles poured on them from the engines on the city walls, and they soon gave up the attempt in despair. From Adrianople they moved on to the capital itself, and were able to plunder its suburbs, made up of the homes of its rich citizens. But the city itself could easily defy them, and they had, in Gibbon's words, merely the satisfaction "of gazing with hopeless desire on its inaccessible beauties." One remarkable incident occurred. Goths and Saracens came into collision; a body of the latter serving in the Roman army under Valens, having sallied out, attacked the besiegers with even more than barbarian ferocity. The Arab cavalry on this occasion overmatched that of the Goths, an omen this of the future Saracenic triumphs. Soon the mighty host retired from the impregnable walls of Constantinople, and dispersed itself throughout the wilder parts of Thrace.

The Eastern empire was safe, though much of its territory had suffered calamities so dreadful that Jerome quaintly describes them as leaving nothing in the countries desolated but "the sky and the earth."

Once more the world was to be united for the short space of a few months under one head, in the person of a man of whom Gibbon says, "that with him the genius of Rome expired." This was Theodosius, the first emperor who humbled himself before a Christian bishop. His submission to Ambrose and his public penance in the church of Milan for his barbarous punishment of a riot at Thessalonica, are perhaps the most familiar facts in the history of the period. Two important events mark his reign; the permanent settlement of the Goths within the boundaries of the empire, and the final overthrow of paganism, at least, of its outward forms and manifestations. His father was a distinguished general, and had suppressed rebellion in Britain and in Africa. But he fell into disgrace, and for some unknown cause was executed at Carthage. The son, who had already governed with ability the province of Moesia and saved it from an inroad of Sarmatians, had retired to Spain, the country of his birth, and thence, like Cincinnatus in the old days of the republic, he was summoned from his farm to be the colleague of Gratian in the empire. Much was expected of him, and it was hoped that he would prove himself a second Trajan, whom in his features he was said to resemble. He had been well educated, and at the same time trained in the simple habits of a soldier, and under his father he had had a wide and various experience of military service. He had first to deal with the Goths, and this he did more by skilful negotiations than by war. It does not seem that he avenged the defeat of Adrianople by any decisive triumph. In fact, like the famous dictator Fabius in the war with Hannibal, he avoided battles, and sought to win advantages and to restore confidence to the Romans without running serious risks. The Gothic chief, Athanaric, worn out with age and fatigue, was glad to make peace with the emperor, and the story is told that he went himself on a friendly visit to Constantinople, the grandeur of which so much impressed him, that he saluted Theodosius as "a god upon earth." There he died, and was buried with befitting pomp. This conciliated the Goths, and the policy of Theodosius was successful. Within four years of the defeat and death of Valens, one tribe of this formidable people, the Visigoths, ceased to be the open enemies of the empire, and were peacefully settled in the provinces south of the Danube, a large colony of them being established in Roumelia.

Theodosius had been brought up as a Christian, and it may be fairly assumed that his Christianity was more sincere and earnest than that of Constantine, who was after all but half a pagan. At any rate, he did not defer his baptism till the close of his life. He was baptized in the first year of his reign, and his next step was to fix the creed of his subjects. Arianism was the prevailing belief of the capital, and the bishop was himself an Arian. The emperor was orthodox, and the bishop was requested to resign, and this he promptly did. In order to establish the faith as defined in the Nicene Creed, the second of the general councils was held in 381, on the imperial summons at Constantinople. It was, however, in reality simply a council of the Eastern Church, though its œcumenical character was subsequently acknowledged. It condemned every phase of Arianism, and in the most distinct and precise terms confirmed the catholic faith. It appears that the most abstruse doctrines of theology were subjects of engrossing interest and daily conversation even among the mechanics and artisans of Constantinople. The people of the city seem to have been as curious and speculative as the men of Athens in St. Paul's time. It shocks us to hear that in the very shops and streets, and even in the baths, the profoundest mysteries of the Christian faith were freely canvassed. This was due not, as we might suppose, to conscious irreverence so much as to a restless and excitable temper. The council itself, as we are told by Gregory of Nazianzus, who presided at it, came to a scandalously turbulent close. The emperor at once proceeded to enforce its decisions by persecution, and penal enactments were passed against all heretics, those especially who at all inclined towards Arianism. But it seems that these rigorous laws were not often carried into effect. Theodosius could be cruel at times, but we may fairly believe that, in his efforts to extirpate paganism and Arianism, he was severe on principle and from deliberate conviction. He probably did not deserve all the praises showered on him by ecclesiastics, still less the preposterous eulogy of one Pacatus, his panegyrist, that "could the elder Brutus revisit the earth, that stern republican would abjure his hatred of kings at the feet of Theodosius." But in many respects he was a good and a great ruler, and at a peculiarly difficult time he rendered the empire important service. He deserves to have gone down to posterity as Theodosius the Great.

It was not till nearly the end of his life that he became for a brief space the emperor of the West as well as of the East. An insurrection in Britain in the year 383 A.D. was the means of ultimately accomplishing this result. The movement was headed by one of the generals in the province, Maximus, who was particularly popular with the troops, and was even proclaimed emperor by them. The rebellion was at once carried into Gaul. Gratian, Valens' nephew, now the reigning emperor of the West, was defeated in the neighbourhood of Paris, and murdered by one of the emissaries of Maximus near Lyons. The provinces of Britain, of Gaul and Spain, now submitted to the usurper, and Gratian's brother, Valentinian, a mere youth, feeling that his position in Italy was precarious, fled with his mother Justina to Thessalonica, and threw himself on the protection of Theodosius. The emperor of the East received the fugitives kindly, and fell in love with Valentinian's beautiful sister, the princess Galla. It seems that his passion for her prompted him to restore her brother to the imperial throne. As soon as he had married her, he decided on war against Maximus. At the head of an army made up of various nations—a mixed host, it is said, of Goths and Huns—he fought a decisive battle at Aquileia, at no great distance from the northern shores of the Adriatic, in the year 394. His rival was given up to him and killed, and now Theodosius was able to hand over the empire of the West to his youthful brother-in-law. But the unfortunate Valentinian was himself soon afterwards murdered by one of his generals, Arbogastes, who had served under Theodosius in the war with Maximus, and who was then commanding the Roman army in Gaul. The man, instead of having himself made emperor (he was but a barbarian), raised to the imperial power one Eugenius, said to be a rhetorician, and his secretary. But the murder of Valentinian was speedily avenged. With the aid of the famous soldier Stilicho, Theodosius, again in the neighbourhood of Aquileia, in the same year, overthrew this new and contemptible rival. It is said that heaven favoured him in the battle, and contributed to his enemy's discomfiture by a violent storm. Now for the last time the empire was united under a single head. For a few months Theodosius was emperor of the East and of the West, but in the following year (395) he died. His two sons, Honorius and Arcadius, had already received the rank and title of Augusti. The first was a boy of eleven years of age, and, with Stilicho for his guardian, he was to reign over the West. It would seem that the father trusted that the principle of hereditary succession was now in some degree recognized, and might be sufficiently respected to ensure something like a permanent settlement.

His elder son Arcadius was to succeed him in the East. With Arcadius begins the definite final separation of the two empires, and what we may properly call Byzantine history. The East and the West soon became thoroughly out of sympathy with each other. At a time when a community of feeling and sentiment was specially needful in the face of the terrors of barbarian inroads, there was positive strife and discord between these two great divisions of the world. Italy claimed to represent the old republic of Rome, and looked down on the East with a sort of contempt which a senator in old days would have felt for Greeks and Asiatics. It was itself again despised as rude and barbarous by the more civilized, if too luxurious and effeminate, inhabitants of the eastern provinces. Already there was a schism between East and West. With two governments, as Gibbon notes, two separate nations came into existence.

From Theodosius to Arcadius there was as great a fall as from Edward I. to Edward II. Arcadius was not unlike the latter prince. He was a poor feeble creature, whom we can hardly think of as a Roman emperor, though of course he bore the title, and was styled Cæsar and Augustus. His appearance was contemptible; he was short of stature and almost deformed; and of accomplishments, such as might be fairly expected in a prince, he seems to have possessed but one, an elegant handwriting. His faults and weaknesses were those of a Persian and Oriental despot. He was ruled by women and eunuchs. Of these last the chief was Eutropius, who rose to the highest honour, and instigated his master to many a cruel act under the pretext of punishing high treason. The man's fate was such as he deserved, and such as history often has occasion to record. A Gothic chieftain had raised a formidable rebellion, and declined all negotiations with the Emperor unless the head of the imperial favourite was delivered up to him. The emperor's scruples, whatever they may have been, were soon overcome by the Empress Eudoxia, the daughter of a Frank, and a lady of conspicuous ability and strength of purpose. So within four years of the accession of Arcadius his unworthy minister was driven into exile and ultimately beheaded.

It is said that paganism declined during his reign, and that the Church could count many converts. The emperor was at least orthodox, and did his best to promote orthodoxy. In other respects the time was dark and dismal. Theodosius knew how to manage the Goths: they were partly afraid of him ; partly, too, they sincerely respected him, and had been conciliated by his judicious concessions. But the weak Arcadius, and the treacherous ministers who directed his policy, soon provoked them. Under their renowned king Alaric they rose in revolt, and poured into Thessaly and the Peloponnese, capturing and plundering Corinth, Sparta, and Argos among its ancient cities. Athens saved itself by a vast ransom. Greece, the population of which had for some time enjoyed peace and prosperity, was so fearfully impoverished by this inroad, that a law had to be passed a few years afterwards relieving it from two-thirds of its customary contribution to the imperial revenue. It was not merely a number of precious works of art which perished, but roads, aqueducts, and public buildings were so utterly destroyed, that the country was condemned to a long period of poverty. The fortifications, indeed, of Constantinople, and the fortunate situation of the city, could defy Alaric, and save it from the ruin which he was soon to bring upon Rome. But the Eastern world, though it arrested the barbarian, was rudely shaken, and sustained fearful loss and damage. The civilization of Greece received a shock from which it never recovered, and the Greek race itself, to the capacities of which mankind owe so much, now grew feebler, and began to dwindle away into insignificance.

Meanwhile the capital presented a striking contrast to all this misery and desolation. Constantinople was plentifully supplied with gold and silver from the regions of Thrace and the Pontus, and its coinage was particularly famous. Its merchants, too, almost monopolised the commerce of the world, and its wealth and luxury seem to have become prodigious. There is every reason to believe that many of the countries under the sway of the Eastern empire were richer and more populous than at present. Along with all this material prosperity there went, according to the writers of the time, a deplorable corruption of life and manners. It is very possible that they may have exaggerated the luxury and depravity of the Romans under Theodosius, though we may admit the force of Gibbon's remark, that the perils of the age and the presence of the rapacious Goths may have inspired them with "the mad prodigality which prevails in the confusion of a siege or a shipwreck." And so, amid the calamities of a falling world, there may have been a progress of luxury which could not have been too severely reprobated. The splendour of the imperial establishment at Constantinople was, unless we have been utterly deceived, grotesquely elaborate and magnificent. It was of a thoroughly Oriental type, as we gather from the invectives of Chrysostom, the most conspicuous figure, perhaps, of the inglorious reign of Arcadius. To his eloquence and earnestness we may, no doubt, fairly attribute the gathering strength and numbers of the Christian Church, a fact which we have already noted. The crying sin of the age was, in his judgment, its vulgar luxury and extravagance. There is a memorable passage in one of his homilies, familiar to all readers of Gibbon, in which, as the historian says, "he celebrates while he condemns" the excessive pomp and show of the court of Arcadius. The emperor's throne was of massive gold; his silken robe embroidered with golden dragons; his chariot drawn by mules of spotless white, glittering with gold, and itself of pure and solid gold, with purple curtains and snow-white carpet, and precious stones of a size to amaze the beholders. Within the impregnable walls of his city the degenerate son of Theodosius knew that he could safely enjoy all this state and grandeur, which must have taxed heavily even the resources of an empire stretching from the Adriatic to the Tigris, and embracing the richest regions of the world. The fact that Huns and Goths, in Asia and in Europe, were menacing its order and civilization, does not seem to have seriously troubled him.

Along with the idle love of vain show and amusement in the capital there must have been genuine religious feeling. By the lower orders Chrysostom was honoured and respected. He had been raised to the archbishopric by the eunuch-minister Eutropius, who had heard him at Antioch, and had much admired his preaching. Base as the man was, Chrysostom thought it his duty to protect him when the rebel Gothic chief, an Arian and a heretic, demanded his life. The archbishop's eloquence saved him at the moment, though, as we have seen, he soon afterwards got his deserts. Chrysostom's great merit was that he did not spare rank and wealth. There was no taint of worldly-mindedness about him, and in such a city as Constantinople this was quite enough to bring him a host of enemies. Of these the chief and leader was the Empress Eudoxia, whose feeble husband was now wholly under her control. Chrysostom's denunciations of luxury might easily be construed into pointed reflections on the emperor, and be regarded as almost treasonable. But, as with John the Baptist, all men counted him a prophet, and with the mass of the population he was a great favourite. A furious riot would have been the result of any openly hostile proceedings against him. The empress endeavoured to crush him by the instrumentality of another ecclesiastic, Theophilus, the patriarch of Alexandria, who seems to have feared that Chrysostom's fame would depress his own rank among the bishops of the Church. To this fear was added a bitter feeling which had grown out of some theological controversy between them, and, on the strength of it, an attempt was made to fasten a charge of heresy on Chrysostom. But the synod which was to consider the matter could not be safely held in the city, and it was summoned to meet in one of the suburbs of Chalcedon. Strangely enough, one of the charges against Chrysostom was inhospitality, although it was notorious that he had dispensed great sums out of his episcopal revenues in charity. A writer of the time, quoted by Gibbon in a note, explains, by way of defence, that Chrysostom never tasted wine, that he often fasted till sunset, that he disliked the bustle and levity of great dinners, and saved the expense for the relief of the poor. But, notwithstanding the bishop's undoubted piety, notwithstanding his wonderful popularity, he was deposed from his see for contumacy, to be, however, recalled within four months by the empress, who is said to have been terrified by an earthquake, which the public voice pronounced a sure sign of Divine wrath. A riot, too, had broken out; a furious mob had threatened the palace, and Eudoxia herself insisted that he should be restored. We see what strength the Church must have already acquired among the masses of the people. It is true, indeed, that he was again banished, and banished finally, through the influence of the empress, whom he exasperated by condemning the honours paid to one of her statues. It was said by his enemies that he began a sermon with the words, "Herodias again rages; once more she dances; once again she requires the head of John." On this occasion the previous sentence of deposition was confirmed at the instigation of the incensed

Eudoxia, and the eloquent and noble-minded Chrysostom died in exile in Pontus. But the day of his departure from Constantinople witnessed a tumult and a fire, in which perished, among numerous other buildings, the church of St. Sophia and the senate-house.

This is far the most striking and significant episode in the reign of Arcadius. It was in 404 that Chrysostom went into his first exile. Arcadius's reign was now near its end. Not one single memorable deed has been recorded of the son of Theodosius the Great. In his last years the provinces of Asia Minor were harried by the Isaurians, a robber tribe issuing from the wild country under the Taurus range, and now becoming famous and formidable. So weak was the government, that it could not stop the incursions of these barbarians, and even Syria and Palestine did not escape their ravages. The administration of the empire seems to have become thoroughly disorganized under this feeble prince. It was a period of every sort of woe and calamity, in which famines and earthquakes and flights of devouring locusts are said to have rapidly followed on each other. All this misery was set down by the unhappy and discontented people to the contemptible character of the emperor and his persecution of Chrysostom. In 408 this wretched reign of outward splendour in the capital, and real feebleness and grievous disaster around it—an inauspicious beginning for the empire of the East—came to a close.

A little boy, eight years of age, the late emperor's only son, who had received the title of Augustus in his early infancy, was the successor of Arcadius. This was Theodosius II., or Theodosius the Younger, as he is sometimes called, by way of distinction from his grandfather. His reign covers the first half of the fifth century, and is one of very considerable interest. His sister, Pulcheria, only two years older than himself, appears to have moulded his character and manners. She may be said to have been his guardian, and practically empress. With ecclesiastical historians she is a peculiar favourite. She devoted herself to a life of celibacy and of charitable works, and her vow was recorded in a golden tablet in the great church of St. Sophia. She was thoroughly orthodox in her opinions, strict and devout in her life, and liberal on an imperial scale to the Church and to the poor. With all this she combined a keen interest in the welfare of the empire, and she made herself really responsible for its administration. Her brother was a mere puppet in her hands. She treated him as a child all his life, and though she taught him how a prince should behave himself on state occasions, and drilled him thoroughly in what we call "deportment," she does not seem to have encouraged him to rise to a position at all worthy of a Roman emperor. In fact, she kept him in leading-strings, and he grew up a poor weak-minded man, of whom the best that could be said was that he was gentle and amiable. "Idle amusements and unprofitable studies," says Gibbon, "occupied his unlimited leisure." It is almost surprising to find that he was fond of hunting. He painted and carved after a mechanical fashion with the most patient industry, and, like his father, he wrote a beautiful hand, which last accomplishment procured him the surname of Kalligraphos—the fair writer. He applied it especially to the illumination of manuscripts. Cut off from the world, he acquired a positive distaste for anything like business, and he signed papers without reading them, thereby often getting credit for harshness and injustice. He was the one last man in the world with whose name we should have expected an important code of legislation would have been associated. The so-called Theodosian Code, which marks his reign, was the fruit of an intelligent reforming spirit now beginning to make itself distinctly felt.

It was the good fortune of the young prince to have also the counsels and guidance of a good minister. The time, as we have said, was a perplexing one, and now the empire was menaced by a host of Huns who had penetrated far into Thrace. Their chief, Uldin, boasted that he would lead them on to the rising sun, but his vaunt soon ended in his having to retire, and even recross the Danube. The prime minister, as we may call him, Anthemius, took prompt measures, which were really the means of saving the empire in the East. On the frontiers of Illyria and Upper Moesia—in what is now Servia—he established fortresses; but his chief and most valuable work was to strengthen Constantinople itself by building, in the year 413, the great walls, as they have been called. These were such as effectually to defy the most furious assaults of mere barbarians.

The young emperor's marriage was the most singular passage of his reign. There is an air of romance about it. His sister of course arranged the whole matter for him, and she chose happily. The lady's name, Eudocia, is one of the most famous in the annals of the Byzantine empire. She was not of royal or imperial lineage, but was simply the daughter of a Greek philosopher and professor at Athens, Leontius, still a worshipper of the heathen divinities. Her original name was Athenais. She was beautiful, clever, accomplished, and familiar with the whole range of literature and science. It seems that she attended—other ladies, we may presume, did the same—her father's lectures, and she also had the advantage of mingling freely in the best society of Athens, among whom culture was fashionable. There can be hardly a question that she was a woman of real genius. To this her father confidently trusted her future, leaving her without any fortune. But for some reason or other she could not find a husband at Athens. In her twentieth year, as it would seem, she betook herself to Constantinople, and was introduced to Pulcheria, then only about fifteen years of age. Soon she professed herself a Christian, and she so charmed her patroness that she became her constant companion, and perhaps stood to her in the relation of a maid of honour or lady in waiting. So she lived for about seven years. But Pulcheria meanwhile had destined her to great honour. With her brother she could do as she pleased, and she decided to marry him to Athenais. He was himself but twenty years of age. It is said that by his sister's contrivance he saw his bride for the first time from the concealment of a curtain, and that he instantly approved her choice. The marriage was at once celebrated, and the professor's daughter, under the name of Eudocia, which she had received at her baptism, became the empress of the East.

The rest of her story is somewhat sad. For several years she was content to live in submission to the wishes of Pulcheria, and to take little or no part in public affairs. After twenty years, when she was not far from fifty, she was the subject of a strange scandal; but it is fair to say that our accounts of the matter are obscure, and the incident we are about to mention is regarded by Gibbon as one which might have found a fitting place in the "Arabian Nights." We may well suppose, at any rate, that it has been exaggerated or distorted by the gossip of the court. The story goes that as the emperor was on his way to church on the Feast of the Epiphany, he was presented by a poor man with a singularly fine apple; that having ordered him to be rewarded on a princely scale, he forthwith sent the apple as a pleasant surprise to the empress, who was, it appears, passionately fond of fruit. The sequel of the tale is certainly very ridiculous. Eudocia, we are told, was too fond of a gouty old man, Paulinus by name, one of the chief officials in the court, and to him she sent the apple. Paulinus, instead of retaining the gift for the sake of the giver, as he ought to have done under the circumstances, took the poor man's view of the matter, and thought the emperor the only person worthy of such a splendid present. The result was that Theodosius on his return from church found his apple awaiting him, and thinking that there must be something amiss, asked the empress about it. By a most unlucky falsehood she replied that she had eaten it. Her gentle husband, who was intensely fond of her, at once suspected mischief. There was, in fact, a scene—old Paulinus was banished, and Eudocia had to undertake a pilgrimage to Jerusalem. But there is another account which attributes her final downfall to ecclesiastical squabbles, in which she and Pulcheria took opposite sides. It is said that for a time she had the advantage, that she won over the emperor to her own views, and that Pulcheria had to withdraw from Constantinople. She was, however, soon recalled and recovered her influence. Eudocia, it is said, ruined herself by procuring the murder of a minister, through whose agency two of her favourite ecclesiastics had been put to death. By this she quite destroyed her position, and lost the state and even title of empress. But the accounts we have are confused and contradictory. She was, it is certain, a considerable author, and wrote paraphrases of certain portions of the Scriptures, and she was something of a poet. In one of her poems she commemorated the victories won by her husband's armies over the Persians. The emperor, it may be presumed, knew next to nothing about this. The most fulsome panegyric was the fashion of the day, and was one of the worst disgraces of the Byzantine court. It was indeed the fitting companion of vulgar show and luxury. There had indeed been in 422 some fighting in Armenia and Mesopotamia between the empire of the East and Persia. But nothing decisive or worthy of commemoration had been accomplished.

The emperor's ambassadors had talked pompously and absurdly about the power and the wealth of their master, the poor inoffensive stripling then shut up in his palace under his sister's tutelage. But the stronghold of Nisibis remained in the enemy's possession, and the conclusion of a long war left nothing but a small district of Armenia to the Roman emperor.

His long reign, indeed, which lasted till 450, was anything but glorious. Its last years witnessed a signal humiliation. We have seen that at the beginning of his reign the Huns withdrew from the neighbourhood of Constantinople to the northern bank of the Danube. But in 441 the "scourge of God," the terrible Attila, brought them back into the southern provinces of the empire, and again unhappy Thrace, up to the very fortifications of the capital, was at their mercy. The cities of Illyria which Anthemius had fortified, among them the strong position of Singidunum, now Belgrade, could not resist the barbarian. The armies of the empire were thrice discomfited by him in the plains of Bulgaria. Amid these woful calamities, in which seventy cities are said to have perished, the emperor took his ease, and life in Constantinople seems to have undergone no change. But the citizens must have been fearfully panic-stricken by the great earthquake in 447, which shattered their walls into a ruin and threw down fifty-eight of the towers. The city may have been still defensible, but we can hardly doubt that in the last extremity it could have been held even against Attila. As it was, however, a peace was concluded, which gave the conqueror the larger part of the Balkan peninsula, and left the empire a mere fragment of European territory. He claimed, in addition, a vast indemnity, which was raised with extreme difficulty. The empire was supposed to be immensely rich, but wild extravagance in the court and capital and an ill-administered financial system had made it poor. We are told that the wealthy nobles and citizens had to sell their wives' jewels by auction, and part with the sumptuous furniture of their mansions, which usually included a semicircular table of solid silver and a dinner service of gold. It seems as if henceforth the empire was to exist simply on sufferance. The young Theodosius was styled indeed a Roman emperor, but of the Roman there was really nothing about him. So far as he had feelings and tastes of his own, he was a Greek of a rather inferior type. Some mental culture he no doubt acquired under his sister's influence, but for the actual government and administration he probably did little or nothing. In fact, he was simply the nominal head of the empire. But it seems clear that he had some able and enlightened men around him. His reign, unprosperous as it was for the empire generally, saw several reforms and improvements. There was a real desire to get rid of burdens and abuses, and to better the condition of the governed. The Theodosian code must have been compiled and drawn up by skilful and learned commissioners. It dealt thoroughly with every branch of the law, and laid down principles with some degree of clearness and precision. We may infer that there were many able and learned lawyers at

Constantinople. The imperial revenue had been raised in a bad and oppressive way; the rich provinces were drained for useless expenditure in the capital, and thus steady industry was discouraged. Liberal concessions were made, and arrears of taxation, which had accumulated during the calamitous periods of barbaric invasion, were remitted. The remission is said to have covered as much as sixty years. One would suppose, indeed, that the ravages of the Huns must have totally destroyed many sources of the imperial revenue. We have already had occasion to note the impoverishment of Greece from the plundering expedition of Alaric and his Goths in the first year of the reign of Arcadius. Some relief for the taxpayer, and some reforms in the methods of levying the taxes, were no doubt among the first necessities of the time. All this was arranged by the Theodosian Code, and it was made easier for any who were oppressed to obtain legal remedies against the wrong-doer. So, while there must have been much misery and confusion in the world, we may believe that the seeds of improvement were being sown, and that there was real progress in the condition of the poor and labouring class. It is said that the system of police was so efficient that the streets of the chief cities of the East were as safe by night as by day. The friendly relation too of the clergy with the people seems to have had a salutary influence. Among the clergy were scholars and men of learning. Their flocks could hear the Scriptures read and explained to them in their own native language. The abstruse theological speculations in which the Greek mind delighted were by no means without their use. If they did not lead to any positive results, we may be sure that their general effect was humanising. It was better for the higher and wealthier class to take pleasure in discussing theological dogmas than in witnessing the last agonies of dying gladiators. No doubt the luxury of the time, in the capital especially, was a scandal and a source of corruption and feebleness; but luxury is, we know, inseparable from wealth and softness of manners, and throughout the East it may have been a civilizing and not a purely demoralizing agency.

A university was founded at Constantinople in the reign of Theodosius—a distinct symptom of intellectual activity. We may conjecture that the emperor's cultivated and energetic sister helped on the movement. It was not the result of private liberality; it was the act of the state, and the university was maintained at the public cost. The professors held very honourable positions, and attained them after having given decisive proof of profound learning and excellent character. A chair in the university was obtained by competitive examination. A professor of twenty years' standing received the title of "count," and became, in fact, a nobleman of the empire. It seems that the officials of the civil service were chosen from distinguished members of the university. Greek was one of the chief subjects of study; Latin was by no means neglected, and there were chairs of law and philosophy. The Eastern world evidently set a high value on learning and culture. Literature was hardly popular in our sense of the word, but religious books were widely read, and religious controversy, as we have seen, excited a keen interest. It is remarked by Mr. Finlay that "the very constitution of society seemed to forbid the existence of genius." The truth is that literature and art addressed themselves to a somewhat narrow circle, which completely set the fashion in taste and criticism. This will usually be the result of imperialism. The writers and artists of the time merely copied good models, and so their works, though not wholly without merit, were apt to be stiff and artificial.

The latter half of the fifth century—indeed, we may say, the whole period from the death of Theodosius down to Justinian—is obscure, from the scantiness of our historical materials. It embraces the reigns of five emperors. After Theodosius, who died in 450 from an accident in the hunting-field, the empire fell to a man strangely unlike his predecessor. Marcian, by birth a Thracian peasant, had begun life as a common soldier, and at the age of fifty-six he was a member of the senate. He had served in wars in Persia and Africa under an able general, Aspar, a man of barbaric origin, whom the imperial minister had found it useful to employ. Pulcheria made him emperor, and, at the same time, for political purposes, her nominal husband. She could do this—so at least she thought—without breaking the vow by which in early life she had bound herself. Marcian's reply to the ambassadors of Attila who came to demand from him the stipulated tribute has made him deservedly famous. "I have iron for Attila," said the soldier-emperor, "but no gold." As we should expect of such a man, Marcian took little interest in the theological disputes which were so attractive to many of his subjects. Yet the Council of Chalcedon was summoned at his instance. The emperor hoped to secure unity for both East and West: as it was, he had to see the Eutychian and Nestorian heresies establish themselves in Egypt and in Asia.

To Marcian, who reigned but for seven years, succeeded the first of the Leos, Leo the Great, as with rather slender reasons he has been styled. His succession was due to the influence of Aspar, who might have been emperor himself but for his heterodox opinions, which were unpopular. He, too, was a native of Thrace and a soldier. He seems in many respects to have reigned well, and to have consulted the welfare of his subjects by carrying out the financial reforms which had been begun under Theodosius. Taxes were lightened, and in cases of public calamity, as when Antioch was shaken by a terrible earthquake, were for a time altogether remitted. He may perhaps have been called "the Great" rather in consideration of his orthodoxy than of his other merits. Although he had been a plain soldier, he knew and recognised the value of learning and education. Once a courtier ventured to upbraid him for giving a pension to a philosopher. Leo's reply was, "Would God that I had to pay no other people than scholars!" He was a really wise and well-meaning ruler. His reign, too, was not without some military glory. The Huns were checked near Sophia, and were glad to make peace. His attempt, however, with the aid of the empire of the West, now much enfeebled, to overthrow the kingdom of the

Vandals under Genseric in Africa, was a disastrous failure. It was undertaken on a prodigious scale, implying the possession of wealth and resources which it is difficult to understand when we think of the losses and calamities which the empire had had to suffer. More than 1,100 ships and more than 100,000 troops are said to have sailed from Constantinople to Carthage. Genseric's fire-ships baffled and confounded this great armament, and the Vandal king again swept the Mediterranean with his fleets. Leo the Great must have seen with bitter disappointment this fatal and ignominious conclusion to his enterprise, and he must have known well, too, that the end of the empire of the West could not be far distant.

It was reserved for his successor Zeno to witness the catastrophe early in his reign. Zeno was called to the throne in 474 on the strength of being the late emperor's son-in-law. He was an Isaurian, and therefore a barbarian in Greek estimation. The accounts, or rather notices, we have of his reign are not flattering, but it is quite possible that they may be biassed. He had at least his share of trouble and misfortune during his reign of seventeen years, and perhaps in disgust and weariness he may have taken his ease and pleasure, as Greek writers say that he did, to the neglect of his imperial duties. Not only had he to see the Goths again under the walls of his capital, and to patch up a miserable peace with their great chief Theodoric, but he was also harassed by palace intrigues and serious outbreaks among the citizens. In the first year of his reign he had to flee from Constantinople, out of the way of an insurrectionary movement stirred up by Verina, the queen-dowager, and her brother Basiliscus. Some few years afterwards he was kept a prisoner in his own palace by his brother-in-law, the grandson of the emperor Marcian and husband of one of Leo's daughters. Theodoric the Goth took advantage of the confusion, and would have made himself master of Constantinople had he not, so the Greek historians tell us, been bribed on a vast scale to retire. Zeno's reign was one of wars abroad and troubles at home, and he really seems to deserve our pity. One good work, at least, he is said to have done for the empire: he raised a force of native troops to save it from the fate which had fallen on the West. The man who did this, remarks Mr. Finlay, could not have been contemptible; and the fact that he did succeed in baffling the formidable Theodoric may suggest to us that history has not done him justice. A barbarian by birth, a heretic, it was insinuated, in his theology, Zeno could hardly have hoped to escape some slander and misrepresentation.

Anastasius, his successor, was elected to the empire in 491 because he married the last emperor's widow, Ariadne. Probably the lady chose him for a husband, just as Pulcheria had chosen Marcian. Anastasius was sixty years of age, and he had been an officer in the imperial guard. Gibbon speaks of him as "a prudent emperor;" a title he deserves, as he contrived by skilful administration to relieve the burdens of his subjects, and to bequeath a well-filled treasury to his successor. One particularly oppressive tax, a poll-tax on men and domestic animals, he abolished with very happy effect; and we may suppose, with Mr. Finlay, that some of the triumphs of Justinian's reign were due in part to these reforms of Anastasius. With a state revenue which he had increased by judicious economies, he executed several public works, thereby no doubt greatly adding to the general wealth of the empire. Hitherto the suburbs of Constantinople had been exposed to every barbarian invader, and had been plundered and burnt by Goths and by Huns. The great wall, forty-two miles in length, stretching, in the form of an arc, from the Sea of Marmora to the Black Sea, was the work of Anastasius. It may, as Gibbon says, "have proclaimed the impotence of his arms," but it probably was the means of long preserving some sort of civilization for the capital of the East, and, we may add, for the world. And it is fair to the memory of Anastasius to remember that his arms were occasionally successful, and that a rebellion in the wild and difficult country of Isauria was thoroughly quelled, his successor in empire, Justin, distinguishing himself in the war. It is true, indeed, that he had in the year 505 to buy a very costly peace from the Persians, who were laying waste Mesopotamia. He was then an old man, but he lived on to ninety years of age, bequeathing the empire, after a reign of twenty-seven years, to a man of humble birth, and also a soldier, Justin. "Reign as you have lived," is said to have been the people's prayer on the accession of Anastasius, and he seems not to have disappointed their hopes, or to have been unworthy of his elevation.

CHAPTER IV.

CONSTANTINOPLE UNDER JUSTINIAN.

SOME time in the second quarter of the first century there were born, in an obscure village —now the city of Sophia—in Bulgaria, three boys of peasant origin. They grew up to be strong, active, and well-proportioned lads, and, like many of their fellows, they became discontented with their village and its surroundings, and marched off together to Constantinople, where they were enrolled in the emperor's guard. All these rose in the service: to one of them was reserved the highest point of dignity, the imperial crown itself. This favourite of fortune, named Justin, was sixty-eight years of age and captain of the guard when the death of Anastasius left the throne vacant. An intriguing eunuch of the court, Amantius by name, proposed to effect the proclamation of a *protégé* of his own by bribing the guard. He made overtures to Justin, who listened, took the money, bribed the guard, and—caused his own election.

He was profoundly ignorant; he knew mankind as a soldier who has spent his whole life in camp might be expected to know his fellow-creatures; he was without any experience of finance, administration, or legal procedure. Yet he governed well, because he had prudence and exercised discretion in the appointment of his officers. His reign is chiefly remarkable because it led to the succession of his more illustrious nephew Justinian, like himself the son of a peasant.

No name in Byzantine history has acquired more general renown than that of Justinian, yet his qualities appear to have been singularly mediocre. The great things that were done for him rather than by him have illustrated his reign, and given it the splendour which belongs to that of a strong emperor. Under him Belisarius reduced the Vandals, added Africa to the empire, seized Italy, raised the siege of Rome, and rescued Constantinople from the Bulgarians. Under him Narses reduced the Goths, defeated the Franks and Alemanni, and governed Italy as exarch. Under Justinian, too, the capital was enriched by the great church of St. Sophia, not to mention five and twenty others; the Byzantine palace was repaired, that of the Heræum erected, and the long walls of Anastasius were rebuilt. And it was under Justinian that the great Corpus of Jurisprudence was arranged and published.

The first act of Justinian, in commencing his long reign of nearly thirty-nine years, was to raise to the throne beside him a woman whose character had been notorious, whose birth was humble, and whose disposition was cruel to ferocity. Theodora was the daughter of a Cyprian named Acacius, who had the charge of the bears at Constantinople. The death of the father left his three daughters destitute. Theodora, the second, became a pantomimist. What else she became may be read in the Secret History of Procopius. Suffice it to say that, unless the historian lies, no more abandoned woman ever stood among the ranks of those who live as the servants and ministers of sin. This woman, deserted by her lover at Alexandria, and reduced to the most abject distress, found her way back to her native city, and there—perhaps repentant, though that is doubtful—earned for a time, and until she attracted the attention of the Patrician Justinian, a precarious living as a sempstress. Like Madame du Barry, Madame de Pompadour, and so many other royal mistresses, she was above all a clever woman. She knew how to fix and retain the affections of her imperial lover. She made him pass a law, under the name of his uncle—for Justin was not dead—by which the old prohibition of marriage between a senator and a woman who had been dishonoured by a criminal, a servile, or a theatrical profession, was removed. And when his uncle died, the new emperor made Theodora empress of the East. In all the annals of self-made women, no parallel success is recorded. Even the Du Barry was never queen of France.

She became in power a woman as cruel as when in obscurity she had been worthless. She loved to retire to the privacy of a palace on the shores of the Propontis, where she could receive, in whatever mood was most congenial at the moment, the greatest personages of the state; where she had the satisfaction of feeling that, in the dungeons beneath her feet, languished the miserable victims of her revenge; where she could receive her spies, who brought her information of every idle word that prince or bourgeois of the capital uttered concerning herself; where she could receive her victims, gloat over their sufferings by scourge or torture, blind their children, confiscate their property, destroy their whole family; and where she could tell her executioners to do her bidding, "or, by Him who liveth for ever, your skin shall be flayed from your body."

An accursed woman. And yet a woman who did good things. While she mutilated, tortured, and imprisoned, she founded an asylum for fallen women, in which she ought herself to have been imprisoned. A brave woman, too. When her husband trembled before the rage of a mob, it was Theodora who armed him with courage. She was proud, avaricious, cruel, relentless, but she was strong.

One of the most singular stories in the chronicles of the city is that of the sedition which imperilled Justinian's throne in the fifth year of his reign.

The races in the circus were originally contested by rival charioteers, who wore red and white colours. To these were afterwards added blue and green. These later colours absorbed the first two in Constantinople. The people naturally took opposite sides at the circus, and then confusing their partisanship in the games with their sides in politics, gradually joined one or other of the two great factions which perpetually troubled and menaced the tranquillity of the city, the green and the blue—one hears nothing more of red and white. Differences in this city of controversy meant religious differences; and a dispute over a theological point could only be carried on by means of fights, murders, and assassinations. So that, when the greens carried their zeal to so great a height as to bring daggers into the hippodrome, and there murder 3,000 of the blues, it was felt by their own party that so strong a step was praiseworthy from a religious point of view: by the other side it was felt that this exhibition of zealous faith must be met by equal earnestness when an opportunity should come. Justinian favoured the blues. They were the orthodox party; they were stronger than their enemies. They began to parade the streets at night, plundering the houses of the greens, and murdering them wholesale. No justice could be had, and it seemed as if the cause of the greens would be extinguished by the massacre of the whole party.

On the occasion of the games held at the Ides of January, the emperor being himself present, the unfortunate greens broke out into open clamour, complaining, with some justice, that they were murdered and pillaged without power of getting redress, and calling on the emperor to grant them justice. For a long time Justinian sat in silence. Then, losing the habitual dignity of his manner, he ordered his crier to inform the greens that they were Jews, Samaritans, and Manicheans. Insulted thus as the worst of heretics, the greens burst into a tempest of rage; they renounced allegiance to Justinian; they cursed the hour of his birth; they loaded him with insults. The blues sprang to their feet; the greens remembered their own day of brief triumph, and, expectant of the daggers, fled from the circus, spreading terror through the streets, while their enemies pursued them. These threatened a massacre of the greens such as would have effaced the memory of their three thousand. It was averted by the lucky incident of the appearance of seven criminals being led to the place of execution. Four were beheaded; one was hanged; the ropes broke by which the other two were hanging, and they were carried off by monks to the sanctuary of the church. It was discovered that they belonged respectively to the blue and the green factions. Were, then, religion and the circus thus to be insulted? Both factions united to rescue the prisoners, to burn down the prefect's house, to massacre his officers, and to open the prisons. The soldiers sent to appease the multitude were fiercely assailed; the women hurled stones upon them from the housetops; the men, in self-defence, set fire to the houses, and a conflagration ensued, in which many of the finest buildings of the city, including St. Sophia, were destroyed. The peaceful inhabitants fled across the Bosporus. For five days the city was in the hands of the factions, whose watchword—which gave the sedition its name—was "Nika," conquer.

Justinian tried concession. He dismissed his principal ministers; he even went to the hippodrome to deplore publicly the errors of his government, but he was distrusted, and so great a clamour was raised that he fled hastily to the fortress of his palace. The mob, masters of the city, seized on one Hypatius, nephew of Anastasius, and, against his will, proclaimed him emperor.

The courage of Theodora saved Justinian, who proposed to fly with the imperial treasures. She found means to communicate with the leaders of the blues and to sow the seeds of jealousy, which soon revived the animosity of the factions. The blues were easily persuaded to turn their weapons against their old foes, and the greens were left deserted in the hippodrome with their unfortunate emperor. Then Justinian took his revenge in a slaughter which assured the greens that their cause was hopeless. Thirty thousand of them were murdered almost in cold blood. Hypatius, with nineteen so-called accomplices of patrician rank, was privately executed: their palaces were razed, and their fortunes were confiscated. For several years the hippodrome was closed.

The conquests and campaigns of Justinian's generals, Belisarius and Narses, cannot find any place in this volume. After the disgrace and retirement of Belisarius the emperor was forced to send for him once more, and entrust to his aged hands the defence of the city. Both emperor and general were old, the former in the thirty-second year of his reign and the seventy-fourth of his age. This time the attack was made by the Bulgarians. The winter had been exceptionally severe: the Danube was frozen, and immense multitudes of the wild tribes of the north flocked down and joined the standard of Zabergan the Bulgarian chief. In spite of Justinian's vaunted fortresses they met with nothing to oppose their southward march; they crossed the Balkans, descended into the plain, and spread in innumerable swarms over the fertile plain of Roumelia. The long wall had been partly thrown down by an earthquake, and the citizens of Constantinople awoke to their danger when they heard that the enemy was within twenty miles of the city, and when they saw the crowd of rustics who pressed in for refuge lamenting the loss of their flocks, the destruction of their homesteads, and the outrages of barbarian hordes who respected nothing—not even monks. In this densely populated city there were about five thousand soldiers in all, and these could not be relied upon. The factions of green and blue were ready enough to murder each other, but they would not go out to face the Bulgarians; and nothing was farther from the thoughts of the enervated Greeks than that they who had so often bought the service of mercenaries should fight for their own safety. Yet it seemed as if now they must either fight or else, like sheep, hold up their throats to be cut.

Justinian ordered the removal of all the gold and silver vessels from the churches in the suburbs of the city, and then sent for Belisarius. Not even the immediate proximity of the danger would induce this most unwarlike of emperors to take the command himself. Some sovereigns, like Louis XIV., love to assume the credit of others' ability; some even venture their own reputation on a campaign; others, like Justinian, openly make use of the best officers and repay them with ingratitude. Belisarius came, and speedily sallied forth with such troops as he could get together. He could reckon on a small body of 300 veterans: the rest had seen no service and had small stomach for the fight. He took with him a body of peasants, whom he set to dig a ditch and throw up a hasty rampart, and at nightfall he lit innumerable fires, to convey the impression of superior numbers. In the morning the cavalry of the Bulgarians advanced to the attack. Belisarius, knowing the weakness of his civic troops, placed them in ambuscade on either flank, while with the guards he received the charge of the enemy. But when the Bulgarians dashed headlong upon the assault, they were met in front by a compact body of disciplined soldiers, through whose lines they could not break, and were assailed on either flank by showers of arrows from the troops in ambush. They turned and fled. The chief withdrew his army. The Bulgarians wasted the summer in the plains of Thrace, but with the autumn they returned with their Slavonian allies, who went back across the Danube.

The people, whose lives had been saved by the skill and prudence of the veteran, surrounded him on his return with acclamations of gratitude. The worthless emperor, whose throne he had preserved after augmenting its splendour by substantial accession and dignity, received him in thankless silence. Belisarius retired to his own palace. Two years afterwards a conspiracy against the life of the aged emperor was discovered. Two of those implicated, forced probably by torture, declared that they had acted by orders of the great general. Belisarius refused to fly while there was yet time, and indignantly appeared before his judges. The case was prejudged; and though the life of the so-called criminal was spared, his fortune was confiscated, and he himself was kept a prisoner in his own house for eight months. His innocence was at length acknowledged, but the course of the old soldier was run. It was not he, as has often been explained, but another and a later general, who in his old age was blinded and set before the imperial palace with a plate in his hand to ask alms.

Justinian died at the advanced age of eighty-three. He was not a great emperor, but he had the sagacity to select the best officers. He was a prodigy of industry; in an age of curiously active intellectual energy, he was philosopher, poet, musician, architect, lawyer, and theologian.

It was in all a most remarkable and illustrious reign —one in which many great questions seemed settled decisively, though none were. Vandals, Goths, Persians, Bulgarians, all were driven back before the "Roman" arms, and nature herself added phenomena to mark the epoch. Comets blazed in the sky, an omen of disaster to some. One earthquake swallowed up a quarter of a million of people at Antioch; another destroyed Beyrout; a third filled up the harbour of Botrys; a fourth was felt in Constantinople for forty days incessantly. War, earthquakes, famine the follower of war — were not these scourges enough for the human race? Yet there was pestilence as well. The spotted typhus, the real plague of the East, that described by Thucydides and Defoe, fell upon the Eastern world. Who can tell how many perished? As in the black plague of Edward III., thousands died daily, but no one counted their number; cities were cleared of their inhabitants, who either fled or died of the disease; harvests were left standing; the grapes rotted on the vines, the fruits upon the trees. When one considers the ruined cities of the East, the roofless temples and churches of Asia Minor, the hundreds of cities in the Hauran, who shall say how much of their desolation is due to the long wars with Persians and Moslems, and how much is due to the great plague of Justinian?

The reigns of Justinian's successors present little of importance to chronicle in the capital itself. Justin II., more vigorous than Justinian his uncle, was afflicted with temporary fits of insanity, which necessitated the nomination of a successor. He passed over his own relations and named Tiberius, his most successful general. Tiberius II. died after a short reign of four years, leaving behind him the reputation of having been the best sovereign who ever ruled the Eastern Empire. His son-in-law, Maurice, with every virtue except that quality, invaluable in a prince, which commands success — an honourable man, a sincere Christian, and full of humanity, has left behind him the record of a brilliant failure. His attempts to reform the army led to a mutiny in which one Phocas, at the time a mere centurion, but popular among the soldiers for his courage, was raised to the chief command. Phocas led his army to the capital, where he found a strong body of discontents ready to receive him. Maurice, deserted by all his followers, fled with his children. He was captured, and after witnessing the execution of his boys, was himself beheaded. It is related of him that when the child of a nurse was substituted for his own he revealed the deceit, choosing rather that his own son should die than that an innocent person, or rather a child innocent of being his offspring, should suffer.

The people of Constantinople soon found that they would have acted more wisely in retaining an emperor who might be wrongheaded, but who was honest and humane. And if Maurice was a bad military emperor, this soldier of fortune was worse. Everywhere the empire was laid waste and devastated by the Persians in the east and the Avars in the north and west. And meantime the tyranny of Phocas exceeded anything ever before experienced or recorded. Two or more successive seditions were repressed and punished with every kind of cruelty. The third, which was successful, was rather a general revolt than a sedition. It was carefully and deliberately planned by Heraclius, exarch of Africa, in conjunction with the leading men of Constantinople, who implored him to save the empire from ruin. He sent his nephew with an army to occupy Egypt and Syria, and his son Heraclius with a fleet to attack the city. Phocas hazarded and lost a single naval battle, fought within sight of the palace. They took him prisoner, stripped him of his imperial robes, tied his hands behind him, and threw a coarse black cloak over him. In this guise they brought him before the conqueror, who reproached him with the manner in which he had governed the empire. To each reproach Phocas answered, "Wilt thou govern better?" One feels a touch of pity for this rude and brutal soldier, thrust for his sins upon a throne, and told to undertake a task for which he had no kind of capacity or understanding. Would any one, he thought, govern better? To govern, to be emperor, what could it mean but the gratification of every desire, and the punishment of your enemies? Would Heraclius govern better?

At least Heraclius understood something of the duties and responsibilities of an absolute monarch. Of all the emperors he was the one most loved by the people of Constantinople. And it seems hardly credible that he should have retained their affections during the calamities and disasters of the first eight years of his reign. Rather may we believe that he was employing those years in preparing for the stupendous effort which he made at the end of that period. The difficulties before him were very great. The treasury was empty, the civil administration disorganized, the agricultural classes ruined, the soldiers actually deserting their standards to become monks, and the citizens of his capital more and more averse to the dangers and hardships of military life. There was but one flourishing portion of the vast empire, the province of Africa. And so greatly did Heraclius feel the danger of Constantinople, that he proposed to transfer the seat of government to Carthage. The patriarch and the people, however, assembled in the church of St. Sophia, and forced him to swear that he would abandon the idea. What would have become of Constantinople had the project been carried into effect? The immediate result would have been the dispersion of the thousands of idle dependants of the court, and recipients of the daily dole of imperial bread.

The magnificence of the city, the splendour of the hippodrome, would have vanished at once. But another kind of greatness might have arisen for Constantinople, such a greatness as, we believe, may await her yet, when she shall become a free and independent city, the emporium of the Eastern trade.

The story of Heraclius—how, like a chivalrous knight, he met the victorious Persian, fought and defeated him; how he restored the Holy Cross to Jerusalem; how he carried the war into the enemy's own provinces, and how he returned in triumph to Constantinople—cannot here be told. He ended his reign in his capital, endeavouring to effect a hopeless task, that of recreating the national spirit by means of a common creed. And with this view he occupied the last years of his life in interminable discussions about the heresies of his time. His Ecthesis, which was designed to answer all religious difficulties and impose a creed upon all alike, only gave rise to new disputes.

Constantine III. and Heracleonas were speedily followed by Constans II., a sovereign of ability and energy. He inherited the dream of his grandfather Heraclius, and endeavoured to secure complete control over the Church. Controversy he silenced, not before it was time. Henceforth, he ordered, let no man argue on any previous theological quarrels. Were all old theological quarrels to be forgotten, it would, he probably thought, be difficult to revive new. In his reign Moawiyah commenced his preparations for the great siege of Constantinople, which he meditated continually The capital became hateful to the emperor after the death of his brother Theodosius, whom he murdered for some unknown cause. Theodosius was in priest's orders. Constans had frequently received the sacrament from him. In visions of the night he saw the spectre of his brother offering him the chalice of human blood, with the invitation, "Drink, my brother." He was himself murdered at Syracuse.

The reign of Constantine IV., who succeeded Constans, was commenced by a very remarkable mutiny. The troops of Asia Minor demanded that the emperor should associate with himself his two brothers, so that in the government of the empire there might be seen a resemblance to the government of the universe. Constantine fought the mutineers with their own weapons. He sent a minister whom he could trust, with instructions to temporize and talk. The emperor, his ambassador was to say, was anxious to meet the views of his faithful soldiers; in fact, he had already intended to make the pious arrangement proposed, but it was necessary to wait for the consent of the senate. Until that could be obtained, nothing could be done. The soldiers appeased, the minister invited the principal mutineers to accompany him to the imperial city. They did so, and were hanged upon the sea shore in full view of their companions.

In the year 672 news arrived that the Saracens were beginning to make preparations on a scale so gigantic that it was impossible to doubt their aim. They collected together an enormous fleet—one always wonders in what dockyards the perpetual construction of fleets numbering hundreds of vessels went on. For what purpose was this fleet got together, save for an attack upon the imperial city? There were signs in heaven, which meant, no doubt, disaster. A rainbow appeared for several days together in March; that was not without meaning. And there was an epidemic in Egypt which meant misfortune, at least to those who caught it. Had the Saracens been as prompt to execute as to conceive their design, there can be little doubt that Constantinople would have fallen, and the history of the East been anticipated by nearly six hundred years.

But one thing, besides this delay, saved the city. A Syrian, named Callinicus, escaped from the Saracenic rule, made his way to Constantinople, and imparted to the emperor a discovery which would multiply tenfold his powers of offence and defence, at least by sea. He had invented a projectile which could be used from ships or from walls—a projectile more destructive, more terrifying, less to be guarded against, than anything yet discovered by the brain of man. It was a fire of so subtle and dangerous a nature, that it would burn on the surface of water, under water, on the stones of walls, and the iron armour of men. It could not be extinguished: neither water, nor sand, nor earth, would put out this terrible fire. It could be projected at short distances through metal tubes, or even in little glass vessels, which could be used as hand-grenades; or it could be thrown by catapults and arbalists, a hissing mass of inextinguishable fire. The secret of this fire was well kept by the emperors, one after the other confiding it to a single engineer at a time, not even the worst being so foolish or so treacherous as to let the secret escape.

In the spring of 673 the Saracenic fleet set sail for the Dardanelles, and passing without opposition through these straits, found themselves before Constantinople. They were strong enough entirely to surround the three sides of the city which face the sea. With the fleet was Calcon, bravest of the Saracens, and Yezid, son of the caliph. But courage was a thing cheaply valued by the fanatic Moslems. What gave them hopes was the presence among them of three old men, the last surviving companions of the Prophet, who had gone safely through all the fighting, and were now among the faithful to animate them, to promise them the joys of heaven, and to recall to their minds a prophecy that whoever was happy enough to fall in the taking of Constantinople, to that sinner should be remitted in full the whole sum of his sins, however many. No doubt there were many among these warriors who felt that, what with the plunder of towns and the madness of victory, the sum of sins to be remitted was sufficiently great. One of them, Abu Eyub, died during the siege, and was buried near the walls: his tomb is still an object of veneration to the Moslems.

The first year's attack lasted for five months. The Saracens lost a large number of ships and men by the Greek fire, which astonished them beyond measure. By means of its use they were probably prevented from coming to close quarters in such numbers as could have made an attack effectual. No doubt, too, their ships were small and light. When the summer was over, and they were no nearer their object, they retired to Cyzicus, which they captured, and made it their winter quarters. Year after year they returned to the attack; year after year they met with the same obstinate resistance, the same calamities from the accursed fire; year after year they had to begin again their military engines. Yet it was not until the seventh year that they finally retired, and then only because a pestilence broke out among them. As the Greek fire had destroyed so many of their ships, they could not embark all their men in their vessels. It is not stated how many were able to crowd on the ships, but the whole number were cast away in a great tempest and destroyed. Nor was the land army more fortunate. The emperor sent after it all the troops he had in the city. The Greeks came up with the Saracens at Cibyrra. The unfortunate Moslems, covered with wounds, starving, lame, and crippled, could make little resistance. It was like the slaughter of sheep.

Thus ended the first Mohammedan siege of Constantinople. Many generations were to elapse before the infidels were to win their prize.

The only other event of the reign of Constantine was of a theological character. The sixth general council was held in the city in the year 680. In this the Monothelists were condemned, and a peace was patched up with the pope.

Justinian, who succeeded in 685, was dethroned, and had his nose cut off. After ten years of struggle he came back again. Mean time there had been two other emperors, both of whom he murdered. Finally he was murdered himself, with his son Tiberius. In him, therefore, the Heraclian dynasty expired. Philippicus, Anastasius II., and Theodosius III. rapidly followed. Their reigns were very brief, and ended with the year 717. The first established the Monothelite doctrines in the Church; the second re-established orthodoxy; and the third is only remarkable for having advanced the fortunes of Leo the Isaurian, and rendered it possible for him to be proclaimed emperor.

CHAPTER V.

THE ISAURIANS.

LEO the Isaurian was a soldier of fortune and of comparatively humble origin, his birthplace being a small city of the Lesser Armenia, near the borders of Syria. When the place was taken by the Saracens, his parents migrated to Thrace. It was prophesied to the boy by two strangers that he should one day become emperor of the East. They conjured him, in that event, to put an end to the idolatry of the empire. This he promised to do, upon which they informed him that they were Jews, and disappeared. So far the miracle-mongers. When Leo ascended the throne, they go on to relate, he remembered his promise, put down the idols, but went on persecuting the Jews. The bearing of this legend will presently appear.

It was under Anastasius II. that Leo was raised to a command—that of the Anatolian Province. It would appear as if he was pushing his way to distinction at the most unfortunate time possible. The state was torn by the conflicting factions of usurpers. In twenty-one years six emperors had been dethroned: military revolts overthrew every army that was raised to meet the Saracens.

Constantinople was threatened by the Bulgarians, who ravaged and plundered under its very walls, while the Saracens invested the city on the opposite shore of the Bosporus. The Saracens, indeed, had now reached their broadest limits. They held Spain in the west, Cashgar and Scinde in the east. To the Caliph Suleiman it seemed a small thing to order his brother, Moslemah, to complete the conquest of this decayed empire, which consisted of little more than a single city ruled by one pretender after another, each after a year or two making way by murder, mutilation, or deposition, for the next.

Moslemah ordered his officers to sit down before the town of Amorium. Leo was the Byzantine general to whom as governor of the Anatolian Province it fell to raise the siege if possible. He wanted time. He gained that time by one of the most singular and most daring feats on record. He visited the Saracen general who commanded the siege of Amorium with an escort of 500 horse only. He invited him to suspend further operations until the decision of Moslemah on certain points could be ascertained, and he contrived a secret meeting with the bishop of Amorium, in which he exhorted him to continue the defence. Then he proposed that they should take him to Moslemah, with whom he would treat in person. The Saracen, willing to present himself with so valuable a prisoner as the governor of the Anatolian Province, acceded. They reached a narrow defile from which a cross road led to the advanced posts of his own army. Arrived there, this wonderful Greek, as daring as treacherous, drew his sword, cut his way with his five hundred, and reached his own camp in safety. What soldiers can withstand the charm of personal courage? Leo's could not. They forced the Saracens to raise the siege of Amorium, and then, following that evil fashion of the time which Leo and his successors were to change, they proclaimed their general emperor of the East.

He accepted the position; he marched upon the capital; he defeated the son of Theodosius III.; he placed the fallen sovereign in a monastery; he made a triumphant entry into the capital; and he was crowned by the patriarch in the church of St. Sophia.

The siege of Amorium was raised and the successful general was on the throne, but the caliph could not believe that the city of Constantinople was any stronger. His brother Moslemah proceeded to attempt that final conquest which should enable the Moslems to attack Europe simultaneously at the east and the west—from Spain and from the Golden Horn. He got together 1,800 vessels of all kinds. He divided his fleet into two portions, of which one was designed to intercept supplies from the Archipelago, and the other from the cities of Cherson and Trebizond. Mean time he passed 180,000 men across the straits, and so prepared to invest Leo by land and sea. Very few details of this siege have been preserved, but it would appear as if the defence was so skilful and so successful that it gave a glory to the name of the Isaurian, which lasted for four generations at least. What is certain is that the Saracens in an attempt to carry the place by assault were hopelessly repulsed by the Byzantine skill in machines and engines; that the attempt of Moslemah to prevent the passage of provisions into the city failed; and that the Saracens' ships were destroyed by fire. Leo, on the other hand, well provided with food and supplies of all kinds, waited with patience within the walls, the spirit of the people rising with every small advantage. The caliph died; the winter proved severe. The Saracen soldiers, unused to the piercing frost, died in multitudes. Their provisions ran short; and when reinforcements arrived in the shape of 800 ships from Alexandria and from Africa, they were manned in great part by Christians, who, dismayed by the wretched plight of the army, deserted in thousands to the Greeks, and informed the emperor of the enemy's weakness. Leo took advantage of this information, and by the aid of his ships succeeded in destroying a great part of the Saracens' naval force. A year and a half after the commencement Moslemah raised the siege. Part of the troops were embarked on board the ships, but the fleet fell in with a tempest and was dispersed. Then the islanders went out after them. In the end five only out of the original 2,600 vessels are said to have reached the shores of Syria—a destruction unparalleled in history. The rest of the army made a a peaceable and safe journey across Asia Minor to Damascus.

Finlay compares this check to the Saracenic arms with that given them by Charles Martel at Poitiers. He sees in the latter a trifling success over a plundering expedition, and in the former a lesson that the limits of Mohammedan rule must at least be those of the narrow seas. Perhaps he is right. And yet the effect in the one case was permanent, while in the other the lessons had to be renewed again and again. But it is quite true that, as he says, "a soldier of fortune, just seated on the imperial throne, defeated the long-planned schemes of conquest of the Caliphs Wezid and Suleiman, and it is unfortunate that we have no Isaurian literature." It is well to mark that the success of 718 was followed up by later triumphs, which completed the destruction of the Saracenic terror until the caliphate passed into the hands of the Abassides. So much therefore must be credited to Leo. There were two enemies to the empire, the Slavonians of the West and the Saracens of the East. Either of these might, during the rule of one of his predecessors, have destroyed the empire. He effectually broke the power of one, and struck terror into the other.

This extraordinary man, however, was not only a victorious soldier, but also a reformer, civil and ecclesiastical. Like Napoleon, he brought common sense to bear upon an intricate and obsolete code of laws. The old Roman code, owing to the interruption of communication and other causes, had been here and there supplemented by local usages. Leo was the first emperor strong enough to prepare and issue a new manual of law, to modify and infuse new energy into the military system, and to control the administration of finance. It was by the changes and reforms of Leo that the empire was enabled, for centuries to come, to withstand and drive back the Moslems.

But the character of Leo has been blackened by his enemies, the priests. He was an iconoclast.

The worship of pictures and images had become among the common people, and especially among the ignorant monks and the lower classes of the capital, not a superstition grafted on to religion, but the whole of religion. If we imagine what London would be were all her clergy ritualists and all her laity under their control, we may realise what Constantinople was in the time of Leo. Holy pictures to be revered and kissed were hung in all the churches ; every house had its saint or its picture. There was no longer any Christ or any God in the minds of Christians, but only for each his favourite saint or his favourite picture. It was not so with those who had travelled among, fought with, or learned the customs of the Saracens. These, chiefly soldiers like Leo, saw with shame the purity of the monotheistic Moslems contrasted with their own paganized Christianity. And one of the earliest reforms of this strong man was the abolition of idolatry. He first ordered the pictures to be raised so high on the walls that they could not be kissed. The islanders of the Archipelago rebelled and sent a fleet with a newly-appointed emperor of their own to attack Constantinople. Leo met these ships with his own and completely destroyed them. He then called a council, which declared against images. The pope excommunicated all iconoclasts. Leo disregarded the excommunication and went on his own way. Rome never afterwards applied to Constantinople for confirmation of a papal election, and the schism was begun which widened every year. The friends of the images were not slow to point out that the wrath of Heaven against the iconoclasts was shown by a fearful volcanic eruption and an earthquake which destroyed part of the walls of Constantinople and overthrew many monasteries (which had been the storehouses of images) and churches where the saints loved to have their pictures hung. So that if the earthquake was sent by the offended saints, their wrath was blind and their curses recoiled upon themselves.

The next emperor, Constantine V., was an iconoclast as determined as his father. It is curious to compare the portrait drawn by monks and priests with that which a critical reader of history has been able to deduce from facts. The fearful crimes which are imputed to him resolve themselves into these: that he drove the ignorant and swinish monks from the monasteries where they lived in idleness; that he denied that any man could be a saint; that he rejected the belief in the intercession of the Virgin; that he refused to believe in the transference of merit. In other words, he had been brought up to reason in matters of religion as well as in matters of politics. He who reasons, regarded from a priestly standpoint, is lost.

The reign began with a rebellion, in which Constantine's brother-in-law, Artavasdes, assumed the crown, seized Constantinople, and was acknowledged emperor by the pope. Constantine waited a year, while he collected his troops and made his preparations. In the battle he routed the troops of his adversary, who fled to the capital. He then invested and besieged the city by sea and land. The people began to starve. Constantine is said to have received refugees into his own camp. The city was taken by a general assault. The usurper fled by sea: he was captured with his two sons; their eyes were put out; they were then immured in a monastery, adding three more to the emperors of the East who have worn out their sightless days in these abodes of sorrow.

The external events of the empire were the long wars with Bulgarians and Saracens, the repression of brigandage, and the improvement of the Slavonian colonies. The internal history of this reign presents a steady progress along the lines marked out by Leo. A general council condemned image worship, ordered the destruction of all holy pictures, and proscribed "the godless art of painting." Again the saints showed their displeasure; once by darkening the sun for five days; once by an earthquake in Syria; once by a winter of great severity; and once by the great pestilence which raged over the whole world.

The successor of Constantine, Leo IV., died in five years after his accession, and was succeeded by a boy, Constantine VI., ten years old, who was ruled by his mother Irene. Then the iconoclasts were persecuted in their turn. Irene called a general council at Nicæa, which entirely revoked the doctrines of that held under Leo. Irene deposed her son, put out his eyes, and crowned herself empress. There was more than the average amount of blindings and mutilations under this woman, who, like most women in power, showed herself callous to human suffering and implacable in her revenge.

The Saracenic wars assumed the character of annual incursions into Christian territory for the purpose chiefly of capturing slaves. Haroun Al Raschid himself, on one occasion, marched across the whole of Asia Minor, and gazed upon Constantinople from Scutari. Irene bought him off by the promise of an annual tribute.

The end of Irene appears like an act of justice. She was dethroned by the grand treasurer, and sent to end her days in poverty on one of the islands. The new emperor, Nicephorus, was not a soldier, but he possessed very great financial capacity, and understood that his surest means of preserving the crown was by the maintenance of numerous and well-disciplined armies. What concerned the citizens of Constantinople most was that he taxed Church as well as civil property, a step which was naturally resented by the ecclesiastics. Nicephorus, too, exasperated the priests and monks by his tolerance in religious matters. He was defeated and slain in an invasion of the Bulgarian kingdom.

In the next emperor, Michael, the son-in-law of Nicephorus, the monks had a man after their own heart. He lavished the imperial treasures on monasteries; he ascribed any success to the intervention of some saint; he decorated their tombs with silver; and when his army was defeated by the Bulgarians, he confessed it was a judgment of Heaven for taking the throne of his brother-in-law. He, too, went to end his ignoble days in a monastery.

Leo, the Armenian, who was elected in his place, had barely time to get himself crowned, before Crumn, the Bulgarian king, appeared before the walls of the city. His army was not strong enough to risk an assault along the whole wall, and he therefore set his soldiers to the work of plunder, in hope of obtaining speedy and favourable terms of peace. A conference was appointed, at which Leo endeavoured to assassinate the king. He failed in the attempt, owing, says a Christian and priestly biographer, to the multitude of his people's sins. Crumn retaliated by destroying the suburbs, and marched away with an innumerable number of slaves. Leo succeeded the following year, by a night surprise, in annihilating their formidable army. The Bulgarian peril thus averted, Leo was able to attend to home matters, which at this period were ecclesiastical. Just as the iconoclasts went to the extreme of attacking even the art of painting, so their opponents went to the extreme of claiming for images the power of working miracles, revealing the existence of treasures, prophesying the future, and raising their possessor to high rank. The soldiers were all, as in the days of Leo the Isaurian, iconoclasts. They destroyed whenever they dared to move. Then another general council was held which abolished image-worship for a second time, and Leo had the moderation and good sense to make no one a martyr. He was murdered in his private chapel on the morning of Christmas Day, and Michael of Amorium, who was lying in the dungeon, awaiting execution, was proclaimed emperor. He, like Justin, was a soldier born in the lowest rank, and it was by his personal influence that Leo had been proclaimed. It is not clear what were the motives which influenced the conspirators in raising him to the throne. He was popular with the soldiers, but among other classes he was known to be lax on Church matters. Thomas of Gazouria, in Pontus, one of the generals, headed a formidable rebellion against the newly-proclaimed emperor. He overran Asia Minor, and, crossing the Bosporus, closely invested Constantinople by sea and land. The siege lasted about eight months. Michael had laid in abundant provisions, and there was no suffering. Two general assaults were repulsed with bravery and success. The fleets of Thomas were destroyed by others raised for Michael, and the pretender had at last to fall back upon Arcadiopolis, where he was presently taken, and, after his limbs had been struck off, was hanged.

Michael endeavoured to conciliate the monks while he despised their beliefs. But by marrying a nun, and, not only that, but by contracting a second marriage at all, he provoked their enmity.

The story of the reign of Theophilus, his son, is a remarkable collection of anecdotes. He ruled like a sultan. The stories about him are like those which are told of Haroun Al Raschid. Unlike the previous emperors, he had been carefully educated. He was a bigoted iconoclast, and he was resolute in his endeavours to purify the administration of justice. He rode once a week to the church of St. Mary at Blachern, in order to afford his people the opportunity of presenting petitions: he ordered striking examples of the punishment of unjust judges. He strengthened the walls, built a hospital, erected splendid palaces. He was an enthusiastic admirer of music, and he cultivated art as he understood art. In his campaigns he was unfortunate, though his valour and military skill were never impugned; but he was unlucky. His last act when he found himself dying was a crime singularly out of keeping with the tenour of his life. To preserve the safe succession of his son he beheaded his best friend and brother-in-law, Theophobus. When the head was brought to him, the dying emperor moaned, "Thou art no longer Theophobus, and I am no more Theophilus.'

This son was only three years old. Theodora, his mother, was appointed regent. In this reign the city witnessed another general council which re-established image-worship, and undid all that had been done before. Like the act of Irene, it was the work of a woman, the regent. Theodora appeared before the council, and offered them her support, provided they would pass an act declaring that her late husband's sins were forgiven. If they did not see their way to that daring statement, she feared that her influence must be thrown into the opposite scale. A way was found, and the sins of Theophilus declared to have been forgiven. Image-worship was brought back into the Greek Church, and there it still prevails. A few years ago we should have laughed at the superstition. Now all is changed. The same danger threatens this realm of England as was averted for a time by Leo the Isaurian. History repeats itself. The dangers of pictures, shrines, and images are always the same; and there are never wanting those who willingly give up the personal responsibilities of the Christian life, and accept in exchange the promises of men who, with images and pictures, bell and book, incense and vestments, assert for themselves supernatural powers, and claim to guard the gate of heaven.

The Paulicians were a kind of Byzantine Quakers, except that they were not meek. They would have no images. If they had priests at all, these did not form a special order of society; they refused to acknowledge the authority of a hierarchy. They came from Samosata, where their founder, one Constantine, had derived his simple system from the New Testament itself. They were driven by persecution to seek among the Saracens the toleration which the Christians would not concede. When Theodora had martyred ten thousand of this inoffensive people, they rose in revolt, joined the Moslems, and finally settled in a secluded country, difficult of access, where they maintained their independence.

A time of persecution for creed is not generally a time conspicuous for elevation of moral tone. This was a period in which all society seemed abandoned to the grossest vices. It would be only a vain repetition to tell of the murders, the mutilations, the tortures, of this reign. Theodora abandoned her son's education to her brother, Bardas, who gave his nephew opportunity for indulging his vices, encouraged him to order the execution of Theoktistus, his financial minister, forced Theodora and her daughters into a monastery, and joined the young emperor in his most shameless orgies. Among the favourite amusements of this most Christian prince was the public burlesque of the ceremonies of the Church. Michael the Drunkard lacked none of the ability of his forefathers: he was successful in his military enterprises, and was popular among the lower classes, who probably knew little enough of court life and its infamies. His reign is remarkable in many ways. First, the dispute between Photius the patriarch and Pope Nicholas. The latter claimed to be absolute master of the whole Christian Church; the former declared that the patriarchs of Constantinople were equal in rank to the popes of Rome. Then, were the newly converted Bulgarian Christians to belong to the jurisdiction of Rome? Secondly, the reign is remarkable for the first appearance of the Russians. Two or three years before they made their first attack, Rurik, a Scandinavian, arrived at Novgorod, and speedily reduced to submission the surrounding tribes. No one knows what motives induced the Russians to threaten Constantinople. Probably on spreading southwards and gaining access to the Dnieper vague rumours reached them of the city's wealth. They suddenly appeared with a fleet of some two hundred small vessels, which might have carried 6,000 men or so, at the mouth of the Black River in the Propontis. They ravaged the country, burned the monasteries of the Prince's Islands, and slaughtered holy monks just as if they had been common people. The emperor, who was on the Asiatic side, and about to commence a campaign against the Saracens, hurried back and speedily put them to flight. The descent was like one of those contemporaneous Danish invasions, in which the invaders came in light ships, prepared to carry off what they could, and escape when their enemy was too strong. It was not an attack or a siege, as it has been foolishly called; it was a foray. And so successful a foray was it, that the Russians were tempted to repeat it a second, a third, and a fourth time. Lastly, this reign is signalized by the rise and early fortunes of Basil the Macedonian.

Basil was the son of a herdsman of Macedonia. He was carried away as a boy by the Bulgarians, among whom he grew up, living on their wild fare, sharing in their wild sports, becoming as handsome as David and as strong as Samson; fearless and skilled in all the arts which fighting races love. He either escaped, or was allowed to return, or fought his way to freedom, and went to Constantinople, where he entered the service of the emperor's cousin, whom he accompanied to the Peloponnes. There, a Greek matron looked on the comely stripling with eyes of love. She gave him money, horses, and servants, so that from a mere stable-boy young Basil found himself able to maintain a certain appearance at his patron's little court. Perhaps it was then, perhaps later, that he discovered and announced the fact of his royal descent. He was, he said, of the blood of the Arsacidæ, the kings of Parthia. Perhaps he believed in his own descent. There are still, we are told, families in the Greek mountains, which claim hereditary descent from officers of the court of Alexander the Great, and believe their own claims. Returning to Constantinople, Basil attracted the attention of the emperor by his dexterity and strength in wrestling, his address in taming a vicious horse, his skill as a sportsman, and his admirable gifts as a boon companion. Michael attached the young countryman to his own person, promoted him rapidly, and gave him the highest court offices. Then Bardas began to grow apprehensive. He was becoming old. He would no longer please the emperor as he had been wont to please; he was not young enough to share as a guest the imperial orgies. And while he looked on Basil's rise with jealousy, he knew that his enemies regarded it as the beginning of his own fall. That event, indeed, happened very soon. Basil and Symbatios, another and a rival favourite, together accused Bardas of plotting against the emperor's life. Michael took no immediate steps; but shortly afterwards, while Bardas in the imperial tent was urging on the emperor to lose no time in the prosecution of an expedition against Crete, Basil and Symbatios fell upon him and murdered him under his nephew's eyes. The Cretan expedition was abandoned, and on his return to the capital the emperor was greeted by a voice from the crowd which cried, " Hail, emperor! You return covered with blood, but it is your own!"

Basil was now rewarded by being proclaimed the colleague of Michael, with the title of emperor. Symbatios got nothing. In revenge he crossed over to Asia Minor, persuaded Peganes, who commanded the army of the

Opsikian Province. Their revolt was unsuccessful. Peganes, who was first captured, had his eyes put out; Symbatios, whose turn came immediately afterwards, had his right hand cut off and his right eye put out. They were then placed before the gates of the palace of Lausus, with a platter on their knees, as common beggars. It is from the miserable end of these two illustrious generals —blind, begging their bread—that the touching story of the last day of Belisarius is probably derived.

While Basil reigned with Michael, the emperors broke open the tomb of Constantine V. the Iconoclast, dragged out the body, which had lain there for ninety years, and burned the remains in the place used for the execution of malefactors. Then Michael, whose drunkenness was bringing on delirium tremens, placed a third colleague, one Basiliskios, on the throne.

After this, it became a mere chance which should be the first to murder the other two. The coolest head, of course, triumphed. Basil it was who murdered the other two while they were asleep after a drinking bout.

This murder ended the Isaurian, and transferred the crown to the Macedonian, dynasty.

CHAPTER VI.

THE MACEDONIANS.

IF Justinian has suffered at the hands of a spiteful writer, Basil has gained by the partiality of his biographers. The groom, stable boy, peasant, who rose to be the companion of an emperor, who married the emperor's mistress, and corrupted the emperor's sister, who murdered his benefactor, who was a bad general, who finally destroyed the ancient Roman constitution and established an arbitrary despotism, appears as the illustrious scion of a royal though fallen race, as able in war as in administration, and as eminent for religious as for political qualities.

We have already sketched his youth and the manner of his rise to power. The incidents of his reign have but little to do with the city, and may be briefly touched upon.

At his coronation he made haste to display his piety by kneeling before the altar and proclaiming that he dedicated his crown and himself to the service of God, who had raised him to the empire. He called a general council of the Church, at which small concessions were made to the Latins. These, however, led to no permanent reconciliation. The emperor resumed some of the lavish gifts made by the drunken Michael to his favourites, and in this way collected 30,000 pounds weight of gold without taxation. He never, indeed, increased the taxes—a policy which largely contributed to the popularity which clung to his race for more than a hundred years. He published first a new Manual of Law, and subsequently a complete new code called the Revision of the Old Law; and he maintained the army in efficiency. The wars of his reign were those which were waged with the Saracens, and a military expedition against the Paulicians. Basil extended the power of the empire in Italy, lost Syracuse, and regained Cyprus, which he held only for seven years.

He received a visit while emperor from Danielis, a Peloponnesian matron, to whom he owed his first rise from the lowest rank of society. She brought him splendid gifts, including hundreds of young men, eunuchs, and girls, for the service of the imperial household, immense stores of rich drapery and woven stuffs, and a service of cups, plates, and dishes in gold and silver. After Basil's death she made Leo VI. heir to her prodigious wealth. One wonders if there were many ladies of the Peloponnese so richly endowed. Her slaves were so numerous that the emperor sent 3,000 of them into Apulia to cultivate the land; and her estates were so vast, that after paying all the numerous legacies, her heir remained the possessor of eight villages.

Basil was carried off by a fever, the result of an accident in the hunting field. The suspicion and ferocity of his character are shown by the fact that he caused the servant who saved his life by cutting him free from the boar, whose antlers had caught in the bridle, to be beheaded. Thus he ended his reign as he began it, a murderer.

He was succeeded by his son, Leo VI., the Philosopher. Leo reigned in comparative tranquillity for twenty-five years. The Saracen fleets ravaged fearfully the seaboard of the empire, and even succeeded in taking the important city of Thessalonica, and carrying off 22,000 of the inhabitants as prisoners. The frontier wars in Asia were still waged with success on neither side; and after seventy years of peace between the Bulgarians and the Greeks, war again broke out with that prosperous nation. It was disastrous to the Byzantine arms. The Bulgarians defeated the troops sent against them, and cut off the noses of all the prisoners. Twice again Leo's armies were defeated before peace was concluded.

Stringent rules were passed during Leo's reign on the observance of the Sunday. The suspension of all civil business on that day had been ordered long ago by Constantine: one by one, exemptions were permitted. During the iconoclastic quarrels both sides were eager to show their piety by scrupulously regarding Sunday. Leo ordered that these exemptions should all be revoked: not even necessary agricultural work was allowed.

The long reign of Constantine VII., who succeeded his father at the age of eight, offers few events of interest connected with the city. His uncle Alexander assumed the regency, but died within a year. The Empress Zoe became regent. Then began the customary revolts and intrigues of generals ambitious to become colleagues on the imperial throne. Constantine Ducas took the lead. He repaired secretly to Constantinople, where the revolt had been already prepared: he was immediately proclaimed emperor, and with such troops as his friends could raise, he hastened to the palace of Chalkê, intending to seize on the young emperor. But the faithful English guards were true to their duty, and the rebels were repulsed after a sanguinary fight, in which 3,000 were slain, including Constantine Ducas himself. Then the Bulgarians gave trouble, their king marching up even to the very gates of Constantinople[1] without opposition. Zoe sent one of the finest armies which ever left Constantinople to carry the struggle into the Bulgarian territory. It was cut all to pieces. Then followed a sort of race between Leo Phocas, the general who lost this battle, and Romanus, the admiral who helped to lose it, for the dignity of co-emperor. It was won by Romanus, whose daughter the young emperor married. Romanus, thus arrived at the object of his ambition, proceeded to name his three sons as joint emperors with himself, putting Constantine in the fifth place. Unfortunately for Romanus, his strength was not equal to his ambition. One of the sons died; the other two, dreading that their father would restore Constantine to the first place,

[1] This demonstration has been called a siege. Simeon, the King of the Bulgarians, appeared before the city twice again, in 921 and 923.

deposed him and sent him to a monastery. They were themselves immediately afterwards deposed and sent to join their father. A pleasing picture is sketched by Gibbon of the old emperor greeting his sons with unbounded satisfaction, congratulating them on their exchange of a temporal for a heavenly kingdom, and cheerfully inviting them to share in his bread of repentance and water of affliction.

Then Constantine VII., who would much rather have remained quietly at work among his books, his music, and his paintings, had to reign alone. He was the most popular of Byzantine sovereigns. It is from his writings that most of our knowledge of his time is derived. He died at the age of fifty-eight.

His son, Romanus II., who succeeded him, inherited the strength and beauty which distinguished the Macedonian line, but possessed a more active and determined character than his father. He might have done great things for the empire, but unfortunately he reigned for eight years only, and died at the age of twenty-four. The one event of his reign was the recovery of Crete from the Saracens.

He left two boys, Basil and Constantine, both infants. The same ambitions were aroused which disturbed the early years of Constantine VII., fortunately without the same loss of life and with a happier result. Nicephorus Phocas, who was crowned emperor very shortly after the death of Romanus II., was a soldier of cold disposition and military discipline. Already of a mature age, he seems to have been of irreproachable morals. Personally he was unpopular. He granted money for festivals and shows with a niggardly hand: he was accused of heaping up treasure for himself. A great scarcity of wheat increased his unpopularity; he issued debased coin, which excited the utmost odium; and, worse than all, he had a constant succession of quarrels with the clergy. For, to stimulate the military ardour of the soldiers, he asked the patriarch to declare that all Christians who perished in fighting Saracens were holy martyrs. The unpatriotic Churchman replied that all war was unholy, and that he who slew an enemy in battle ought to be deprived of the sacraments for at least three years. Nicephorus also restrained the growing passion for founding monasteries: he prohibited the foundation of any more, and declared void all testamentary donations to the Church.

The campaigns of this soldier prince were fought far from his capital. They were successful and honourable. He was murdered after a reign of six years by his nephew, John Zimiskes, instigated by the Empress Theophano, the widow of Romanus II., who had been suspected of poisoning her father-in-law and her husband. The new emperor, who began his reign, like Basil, by a murder, was as able as Nicephorus and far more popular. The great event of his reign was the Russian war.

We have already mentioned the first appearance of the Russians before Constantinople in 865. After the defeat of their invasion the Russians opened up a correspondence with Constantinople, began a trade which grew yearly more extensive, and invited Christian missionaries into their country. Numerous Russian traders took up their residence in Cherson and Constantinople. Russian sailors shipped themselves in the Byzantine fleets. These friendly relations were interrupted, as friendly relations between countries always are interrupted, by the desire of a prince to distinguish himself. It was in the year 907, when Oleg was regent during the minority of Igor, the son of Rurik. He collected 2,000 vessels and made a plundering incursion, called a siege by some writers, in the neighbourhood of Constantinople. Leo bought them off. The next attack was in 941, when Igor made an incursion with "innumerable" vessels. The Russians landed here and there, pillaging, murdering, torturing. Their skill in torture was admirable: priests, especially, were distinguished by having nails driven into their heads. It is satisfactory to learn that an insignificant force of fifteen vessels, armed with the Greek fire, was sufficient to destroy this immense fleet. Igor escaped with a few boats only. Another Russian invasion was projected which came to nothing. Igor being subsequently murdered, his widow Olga became regent for their son Swiatoslaff. She became a Christian. Then the Byzantines began to consider how they could play off Russia against Bulgaria. Nicephorus persuaded Swiatoslaff to invade Bulgaria, which was done with a result exceeding the Greek emperor's design, for the Bulgarians were entirely defeated, and their country occupied by the Russians. Then Nicephorus took the side of the conquered: it was not at all a part of his programme that Russia should be a powerful neighbour separated only by the Balkans. Bulgaria was recovered. Nicephorus was murdered. Swiatoslaff returned to Bulgaria with 60,000 men: he concluded an alliance with Hungarians and Patzinaks, crossed the Balkans, and dreamed of the conquest of Constantinople. That was, however, a dream destined to be left for the Russian imagination for many centuries to come. The Russians advanced as far as Arcadiopolis, where they were defeated by the general Bardas Skleros, and retired behind the mountains. Early in the following spring John Zimiskes, sending a great fleet to hold the Danube and cut off communications, crossed the Balkans, long before the enemy expected him, and falling upon the Russians unexpectedly, defeated them in a series of hard fought battles. Swiatoslaff escaped with the remains of his army, but fell into the hands of the Patzinaks, whose prince made a drinking cup of his skull, writing upon it a moral reflection, "He who covets the property of others, often loses his own." Few subsequent Russians appear to have laid this moral to heart.

There is little or nothing else of metropolitan interest in the reign of John Zimiskes. He died—he is said to have been poisoned—in his fifty-first year, and was succeeded by the two young princes, Basil II. and Constantine VIII.

Basil seems to have inherited part of the character of the founder of his dynasty. But he possessed a greater share of military genius. Like the first Basil, he was severe, rapacious, and cruel: unlike him, he was a man of pure and high morality. His reign—for his brother counted as nothing in the empire—began with the revolt of a general. We will not describe the suppression of this revolt. Enough that it was suppressed, and that, in great measure, by the prudence and skill of the young emperor.

Basil passed the whole of a long and vigorous reign in arms. He extended the boundaries of the empire on every side; under him it arrived at the culminating point of its greatness. He was the greatest of the Macedonian dynasty, and perhaps the greatest of all the emperors. But he has left nothing behind him, but a chronicle of wars and the title, "Slayer of the Bulgarians." He died at the age of sixty-eight.

Constantine VIII., his brother, three years younger, reigned three years alone. He was an Oriental caliph; his brother was a soldier. He spent his time among musicians and dancing-girls; Basil in the camp. Constantine succeeded to the throne after a tolerably long life spent entirely in amusements. He could not expect to live long. Who was to succeed him, and who would govern for him while he lived?

He had three daughters; one was already in a convent, two were unmarried. Of these two Theodora refused absolutely to marry; Zoe, already forty-eight years of age, consented to espouse Romanus Argyrus, whose own wife kindly retreated to a convent, and her husband was crowned emperor as Romanus III. two days before her father died.

The twenty-nine years which follow this marriage, and finish off the Macedonian dynasty, are the shameful history of an old woman's successive husbands, and the incapacity of two old women.

Romanus III. was sixty; his wife Zoe was forty-eight. There were no children. The emperor was indefatigable in all religious observances. He endowed monasteries, decorated churches, and obtained permission to rebuild the Church of the Holy Sepulchre at Jerusalem, which had been destroyed by the Caliph Hakem in 1010. But there was no heir to the throne. Then there were jealousies about Theodora; there were conspiracies in the capital; there were defeats in the field; there were earthquakes, famines, and pestilences; and after six years of uneasy and anxious splendour, Romanus III. died.

Zoe, now fifty-four years of age, but still anxious for an heir, lost no time in placing a new emperor on the throne. Michael IV. was married to Zoe, and proclaimed emperor on the day of Romanus's death. Still there were no children, and the unhappy emperor, who had been a money-changer and a menial, suffered from epileptic fits. There were more seditions in this reign, though the military power of the empire was maintained. Michael IV., who possessed many noble qualities, died after a reign of seven years.

Zoe was now in her sixty-second year. It was absurd to look any longer for the miraculous intervention of Heaven. She resolved to have no more husbands, and named as emperor the nephew of Michael IV. He repaid his benefactress by sending her to a monastery. And then the people rose in fury. Michael was dethroned; his eyes were put out, and he was sent to pass the remainder of his life in a monastery, perhaps the same in which the sons of Romanus I. were still dragging on repentant days.

Zoe and Theodora reigned together. But Zoe was jealous of the superior abilities of her sister. She chose another husband in order to destroy her influence. Constantine Monomachus, of whom very little is known, except that he was openly and shamelessly profligate, had a beautiful mistress whom he brought with him to Constantinople, and with whom he appeared in public —a Christian emperor with two empresses.

The emperor, however, had some glimmerings of conscience. He built hospitals and houses of refuge for the good of his own soul: for the same reason he advanced literary men to posts of distinction—a salutary device which has not commended itself to modern princes who are also sinners—and he completed the rebuilding of the Church of the Holy Sepulchre.

Let us pass over the history of the various revolts which mark this period. Among them was one which led to a siege—which does not appear to have been serious—of the capital.

In the year 1043 began a three years' war with the Russians, which ended in the defeat of the latter. As usual, the Greek fire turned the scale. In the eastern provinces, as well as the western, the empire suffered grievous disasters.

Zoe died in 1050, at the age of seventy. Constantine survived till 1054. Theodora then ruled alone for two years. She was the last of the Macedonian dynasty. At seventy-six years of age she named an emperor. It was Michael Stratiotikos, an old decrepit general. He succeeded, under the title of Michael VI. He was speedily deposed, and was allowed to retire to his own private house, where he died a year or two later.

CHAPTER VII.

THE COMNENANS.

THE events which closed with the fall of the last emperor nominated by a princess of the Macedonian dynasty were due to a remarkable change in the social relations of the empire. There had gradually arisen a rich territorial aristocracy—we have seen how rich was a single heiress of the Peloponnese—who lived much on their own estates, which they personally superintended, and where they were themselves seigneurs, like the great barons of Western Europe. And these nobles drifted perpetually more and more away from the crown. They saw how this prize fell not to any of their own equals, but to soldiers of fortune, servants, and favourites; and they saw the highest military commands entrusted to eunuchs of the imperial household. Of late the corruption of the court, the lamentable and ridiculous spectacle of Zoe marrying one husband after another, and the weakening of the central government, disgusted these lords to the point of forcing them into a conspiracy for an overthrow not only of the actual emperor but for the establishment of a new government, with a more definite order of succession. Certain disturbances, and the unpopularity of the old emperor, precipitated the movements of the conspirators One battle only was fought, and Isaac Comnenus mounted the throne.

The House of Comnenus pretended, like most great Byzantine families, to be descended from a Roman stock. The first Comnenus who appears in history was Manuel, a favourite of the Emperor Basil II. He left two sons, Isaac and John: their family estates were on the Asiatic side.

During the administration of the Macedonians, and especially during the thirty years of confusion when Zoe and Theodora held the reins, the strength of the empire had steadily deteriorated. From many causes the capital was ceasing to be looked upon as the real centre of authority and administration. The roads, which once gave an easy means of communication, had been neglected or broken up; the census and great survey of the empire, which for eleven centuries had been carefully renewed every fifth year, so that there was always ready to hand full information on every province, was allowed to be dropped, perhaps from this very difficulty, the want of roads; the direction of public affairs had been transferred from the great families to the stewards of the imperial household, and these men gave the lower offices of the state to their own friends, so that the organisation of the departments was destroyed. There were no longer councils of state; there was only a cabinet of secretaries. Distant fortresses, harbours, and outposts were neglected, in order that the imperial household might be maintained in greater splendour; the pageants of palace, hippodrome, and church, became daily more magnificent; worse than all, the money, owing to the depopulation of the agricultural districts and the increased difficulty of finding mercenaries, had already entered on its rapid course of deterioration. These evils were too great to be remedied; yet Isaac Comnenus in his short reign of two years bravely attempted to meet and defeat them.

Immense sums had been lavished on favourites. Isaac resumed these grants. Immense sums had been given to monasteries, which were now what the monasteries of France became in the eighteenth century, homes where the cadets of rich families lived in ease and luxury. Isaac took all this money back and granted a pension to each monastery proportioned to the number of monks. Crowds of courtiers had received nominal rank in the army and drew real pay: Isaac deprived them all. In the midst of his reforms he was called away to defeat an invasion of Hungarians, and on his return, being seized with a dangerous illness, and believing himself to be dying, he named a successor and retired to a monastery.

Much of Isaac's good work was undone by the weakness and avarice of the man who succeeded him, Constantine X., of the family of Ducas. He allowed the mountainous country of Armenia to be overrun by the Turks, and by this folly opened the whole of Asia Minor to the Mohammedan arms and religion.

A great earthquake alarmed the East during this reign; walls of cities, public buildings, and churches were overthrown. Among the buildings was the ancient temple of Cyzicus, the columns of which were monoliths seventy-five feet high and twenty-five in circumference, and the ancient church of Nicæa, in which had been held the first general council of the Christian Church.

Constantine reigned for eight years. He left the guardianship of his three sons to Eudocia his wife, and exacted from her a written promise, which was deposited in the hands of the patriarch, that she would not marry again.

It was impossible for her to keep that promise. She coaxed the document out of the hands of the patriarch, pretending that she was about to marry his own nephew; and having got it back, she deceived him by naming as her husband one Romanus Diogenes, who, at least, enjoyed a reputation for valour and popularity with the army. He soon made himself unpopular in the capital by endeavouring to take up again the reforms of Isaac. He suppressed the extravagant displays of the court; tried to revive the discipline of the army; grudged the money spent in the circus and the shows; and restrained the peculations of his officers. Had he been fortunate in war he might have overridden the discontent caused by these measures; but of all brave soldiers, Romanus was the most unfortunate. He was betrayed by one of his generals, Andronicus Ducas, in what should have been a signal victory over the Seljouk Turks, he himself, after fighting like a hero, was wounded and taken prisoner. The emperor of the East was brought before the sultan and thrown upon the ground, while the victor placed his foot upon the neck of his prisoner. That was part of the bitterness of defeat. Yet Alp Arslan, the sultan of the Seljouks, did not retain his prisoner, but concluding a treaty of peace with him, let him go.

The news of his defeat and captivity produced at Constantinople exactly the same effects which the news of Sedan in 1870 produced at Paris. The empress had to fly to a monastery; the emperor was dethroned; John Ducas, the Cæsar, became the real sovereign in the name of young Michael, who was now proclaimed the ruling emperor. The unfortunate Romanus, attempting to fight his way back to his throne, was defeated, captured, and forced to resign. His safety was guaranteed, but no guarantee could prevent the Cæsar from wreaking his revenge upon his enemy by putting out his eyes. They left him without an attendant to dress his wounds, and the miserable man died in the greatest extremities of agony. Before death he collected what little money he could and sent it to his generous victor, Alp Arslan. "I am dethroned," he said, "and dependent upon others. I send you all that I have, as a proof of my gratitude."

At the same time the empire lost its last hold upon Italy when the four cities which still acknowledged the rule of Constantinople, Otranto, Tarentum, Brindisi, and Bari, were taken by Robert Guiscard.

The next few disgraceful years must be passed over rapidly. They present a dreary monotony of rebellion, murder, and defeat. Michael VII. spent his time in idle rhetorical exercises and writing iambics. The Turks extended their ravages to the very walls of Nicæa and Nicomedia. A minister, whose only principle was that of remaining in power, lavished on the court, on the courtiers, on the slaves, all the money that could be extorted from the diminished provinces of the empire. Famine and pestilence visited the cities. The Bulgarians resumed their independence. An Armenian, named Philaretos, claimed the title of emperor in Asia Minor, and was bought off with the safer dignity of Duke of Antioch. Alp Arslan consolidated his conquests in Asia by converting the agricultural serfs, who had hitherto cultivated the soil for the great landowners, into independent proprietors. The Cæsar, John Ducas, revolted, and called himself emperor. He was only put down by an alliance between Michael and the sultan of the Seljouks, and this alliance was naturally bought at a heavy price. Then two nobles simultaneously took up arms and usurped the imperial title. One of them, Nicephorus Bryennius, in Europe, raised an army of foreign mercenaries, with which he advanced to the walls of Constantinople, which he would easily have taken had it not been for his imprudence in allowing his troops to ravage the suburbs. This so exasperated the people, that Michael was enabled to force his retreat. The other, Nicephorus Botaneiates, obtained the assistance of the Seljoukians, was welcomed at Nicæa, and then received the welcome intelligence that Michael had been dethroned, and was now in a monastery, quietly writing more iambics, and no doubt much happier than when he was trembling on the throne. He was allowed to remain in peace, and even rose in the Church to be bishop of Ephesus.

The new emperor was now old: he was not, however, worthy on that or any other account of respect. He reigned for three years, leaving his generals to put down the rebellions which constantly threatened his throne, and living with his courtiers a life of shameful profligacy. Alexius Comnenus, the first general of the empire, was driven to revolt by discovering a conspiracy to deprive him of his command and to put out his eyes. He was joined by John Ducas, George Palæologus, and others. He found himself at the head of a numerous, if badly disciplined, army. He had the reputation of being the best among the soldiers; he was the nephew of that Isaac Comnenus whose reign was still remembered by the troops. He was proclaimed emperor, and he prepared to besiege the city.

The army of the rebel Alexius consisted of Slavonians, Bulgarians, and Greeks, in the service of the great families of Comnenus, Palæologus, and Ducas. The rebellion was in no sense national. The people, indeed, during this period of anarchy, were passive. The capital was defended by those trusty Varangians, who never failed in their fidelity to the reigning emperor, and by a legion called the Chomatian. On the Asiatic side was another rebel, Melissenos, with an army composed chiefly of Seljouk Turks. Could the old emperor have been persuaded to make terms with him, and nominate him his successor, the story of Alexius would have been as the story of Nicephorus Bryennius, or that of any other of the rebel pretenders. But he procrastinated.

Alexius saw that there was no hope of taking the city

by storm, but treachery might help him. There was a captain of German mercenaries named Gilpracht, who held a tower in the Blachernian quarter, which commanded the Charsian gate. They found means of bribing him. At night George Palæologus was admitted into the gate, and his troops immediately took possession of the towers adjoining, and poured into the streets of Constantinople. Here the advantage was nearly lost as soon as gained, the soldiers dispersing themselves about the streets, plundering and murdering. Alexius was left with his partisans almost alone, and had the Varangians known, they could easily have seized the leaders and put an end to the revolt. But they did not know. Palæologus got possession of the fleet; the emperor abandoned his army, fled to the Church of St. Sophia, and offered to resign the crown. Alexius entered the palace, and, perhaps because he could not help it, gave up the city to sack. It is difficult to say whether the city suffered more at the hands of its own countrymen, so to speak, or at the hands of the Latins, when, a hundred years later, Dandolo gave up the city to the license of Frank and Flemish soldiers.

The character of Alexius I. has been drawn by the partial hand of his daughter. Her estimate has not been accepted by subsequent historians in the same admiring spirit. He brought to support a position of the greatest danger and difficulty a mind crafty beyond all precedent, a mind which rejoiced and gloried in dissimulation, a mind which habitually preferred tortuous to straight ways. We cannot follow him through the vicissitudes of his reign, which belong to the history of the empire rather than that of the city. He successfully escaped the great danger of that attack upon his capital which was meditated by Robert Guiscard in imitation of William the Conqueror's conquest of England. He broke the power, after many ineffectual efforts, of the barbarous Patzinaks, who invaded him from the north, and he carried on with varying success the never-ending war with the Turks. The prodigality and reckless expenditure of the court, the multiplication of offices, and the necessity of amusing the people with expensive shows, obliged him to disband the greater part of his army after every campaign, and to commence each new enterprise with newly levied troops. He debased the coinage; was conspicuous, even in a superstitious age, for his superstition; burned heretics, to the great joy of his subjects in the capital; alternately protected and repressed astrologers; invented new titles to secure the allegiance of his courtiers; and reigned a despotic monarch among a crowd of pensioned relatives, who stood near the throne but enjoyed no power.

To the citizens of the capital, the greatest event of the reign was, of course, the arrival of the Crusaders. It is a thrice-told tale. First came the multitudes of Peter the Hermit and Walter the Penniless, with swarms of women and children. Thousands of them had perished long before the expedition drew near Constantinople. But though only 7,000 reached the city with Peter, the numbers continually grew by the arrival of fresh bands, as helpless, as poor, and as wanting in discipline. They were despatched as quickly as possible across the Bosporus, where they were at once cut to pieces before Nicæa. But then came the great armies under Hugh de Vermandois, Robert Duke of Normandy, Robert Count of Flanders, Stephen Count of Blois, Godfrey of Bouillon, Bohemond, son of the dreaded Robert Guiscard, Tancred, and Raymond Count of Toulouse. These came prepared to march through the city as through a conquered state; to fight their way through, or to treat with the emperor. Alexius dissembled his fears, received them with friendship, witnessed without reproach their lamentable ignorance of the court ceremonials, listened to their incessant talk, which seemed strangely undignified to the slow and deliberate Byzantine, who spoke as if his words carried weight, and were not to be heedlessly uttered; and at last, after agreeing to supply the Crusaders with provisions at reasonable prices, to give them an auxiliary force, and to protect all pilgrims, had the satisfaction of seeing them depart across the narrow seas. Probably, from long experience with Asiatic deserts, Asiatic summers, and Mohammedan warriors, it appeared more than probable to the emperor that most of these gallant soldiers would never be able to come back again. This, indeed, proved the event. Of course, Alexius never carried out any portion of the treaty.

One is tempted to ask what the future of Constantinople might have been, had such a monarch as Romanus IV. or Basil II. been on the throne, and had the emperor, instead of distrusting and betraying, frankly joined his troops with those of the Franks, and taken his share in the recovery of the East, Asia Minor, and Armenia.

The successor of Alexius is described as possessing every virtue which becomes a Christian as well as a sovereign. He reigned five and twenty years. He made himself popular in his capital by his military successes. The people saw with satisfaction an increase in the imperial revenues, and therefore in their own material prosperity. He gave up his father's practice of disbanding his forces after each campaign, ceased to rely on the Byzantine militia, and trained his soldiers carefully as professional soldiers, not as volunteers or as militiamen. Naturally, therefore, his armies were composed entirely of foreign mercenaries, of Slavonians, Bulgarians, Patzinaks, Comans, and Turks. John, however, seems to have failed in turning his victories to the best advantage. Perhaps he despaired of improving the ruined roads, rebuilding the broken bridges, and reviving the desolate cities which everywhere mocked the magnificence of Constantinople: perhaps he found no time in the multiplicity of his campaigns. His sister, Anna Comnena, who with his mother conspired against him, did not write his life or exploits. Yet two historians have handed them down, and if we know little personally of this prince, we know enough to be assured that he had none of his father's duplicity, and relied on honest fighting for the defence of his state.

John was succeeded by his son Manuel, who possessed his father's headlong courage without his prudence. He was always, it is true, ready to fight, but he preferred a tournament to a battle, and lavished the treasure of the empire on the unbridled indulgence of every passion. But at the commencement of his reign Manuel was probably the tallest, the most handsome, and the strongest man in his own dominions. Never was seen so splendid a prince. He wore armour heavier than an ordinary man could lift; he carried a heavier spear and shield than even any Norman; he could tear a stirrup in two with his hands. As he had the strength, so he had the vices of the Latins, whose society he courted, and with whom he intermarried. He drank wine to excess, and spent a large part of his time in feasting. Yet he far surpassed the ignorant Westerns in learning; like all the Greeks, he could argue about theology; he interfered with the decisions of the synods; and understood the practice and science of surgery.

The following is an account of the city in the reign of Manuel, given by a contemporary traveller.

The circumference of the city of Constantinople is eighteen miles, one half of the city being bounded by the continent, the other by the sea, two arms of which meet here, the one a branch or outlet of the Russian, the other of the Spanish, sea. Great stir and bustle prevail at Constantinople, in consequence of the confluence of many merchants, who resort thither, both by land and by sea, from all parts of the world, for purposes of trade—merchants from Babylon and Mesopotamia, from Media and Persia, from Egypt and Palestine, as well as from Russia, Hungary, Lombardy, and Spain. In this respect the city is equalled only by Bagdad, the Mohammedan metropolis. At Constantinople is the place of worship called St. Sophia, the metropolitan seat of the pope of the Greeks, who are at variance with the pope of Rome. It (St. Sophia) contains as many altars as there are days in the year, and possesses countless riches, which are augmented every year by the contributions of the two islands and the towns and villages adjacent. All the other places of worship in the whole world do not equal St. Sophia in riches. It is ornamented with pillars of gold and silver, and with innumerable lamps of the same materials. The hippodrome is a public place near the wall of the palace, set aside for the royal sports. Every year the birthday of Jesus of Nazareth is celebrated there with public rejoicings. On these occasions there may be seen there representations of all the nations, with surprising feats of jugglery. Lions, bears, leopards, and wild asses, trained to fight, are also exhibited. All these sports, the equal of which can nowhere be seen, are carried on in the royal presence.

Manuel has built a large palace for his residence on the seashore, near that built by his predecessors, and to this edifice is given the name of Blachernes. The pillars and walls are covered with pure gold, and all the wars, the ancient as well as his own, are represented in paintings. The throne in this palace is of gold, ornamented with precious stones: a golden crown hangs over it, suspended by a chain of the same material, so as to admit the emperor to sit beneath it. This crown is ornamented with precious stones of inestimable value. The diamonds are of such lustre that they illumine the room. Other objects of curiosity are also here, the which it would be impossible to describe adequately. The tribute brought to Constantinople every year from all parts of Greece consists of silks, purple cloths, and gold, and it fills many treasuries. These buildings are equalled nowhere else in the world. It is computed that the tribute of the city alone amounts every day to twenty thousand florins, arising from hostelries and bazaars, and the duties paid by merchandise arriving by land and by sea. The Greeks who inhabit the country are exceedingly rich, possessing great wealth in gold and precious stones. They dress in garments of silk, ornamented with gold and other valuable decorations. They ride on horses, and appear like princes. The country is rich, producing all sorts of delicacies, as well as abundance of corn and meat and wine. The people are skilled in the Greek sciences, and live in comfort, every man "under his vine and under his fig-tree." They hire soldiers, whom they call barbarians, out of all nations, for their wars with the sultan of the

Zogarmion, or Turks. They have no martial spirit themselves, but, like women, are unfit for warlike enterprises.[1]

The long reign (thirty-seven years) of Manuel, which terminated, however, in the emperor's death at the comparatively early age of fifty-eight, was chiefly occupied with wars and campaigns. Few of these have much to do with Constantinople itself, except in so far that to find money to satisfy the claims of his soldiers as well as the extravagant expenditure of the court, Manuel was compelled to have recourse to every kind of fiscal oppression and rapacity. And while the external policy of the emperor was guided by a desire to ensure safety and to gain renown, the internal was actuated solely by the necessity to maintain the imperial revenue. It was with this view that he made the treaties with Pisa and Genoa, which partly counteracted the effect of the concessions granted to Venice. It is a curious chapter in the history of Constantinople.

Partly in gratitude for their help in the Norman War, partly from some idea of policy, Alexius I. had conceded to the Venetians privileges which promised to place in their hands the principal trade of the capital. Certain merchants of Amalfi, when their city was taken by the Normans, went to Constantinople and formed a sort of colony there. Alexius compelled these Amalfi people to pay tribute to the Venetians ; he gave them a whole street of warehouses ; he exempted their merchandise from custom duties ; and he permitted them to trade throughout the whole empire as far as Constantinople and the

[1] Benjamin of Tudela.

Black Sea. In other words, it would seem as if, for some purpose of his own, Alexius favoured the Venetians at the expense of his own subjects. But the interests of the emperor were rather those of the court than of the capital. The concessions to Venice were not altogether ruinous. The emperor excluded all foreign ships from the Black Sea; he retained the monopoly of the grain trade, and he exercised control over the rents of shops and warehouses. It may be that Alexius, who certainly would give nothing unless a more than fair equivalent was ensured him, saw in these concessions the introduction of greater enterprise, more activity, and a larger trade. Towards the end of his reign he concluded a commercial treaty with Pisa also. This was renewed by Manuel, who also made a treaty with Genoa. These treaties were doubtless designed to check the growing arrogance of the Venetians, who began to think themselves entitled to the whole of the trade of Constantinople. Manuel granted his allies the right of establishing a factory, erecting a quay, and building a church. He fixed a duty of four per cent. on all goods exported or imported; both Pisans and Genoese were excluded from the Black Sea; and in case of shipwreck, property and sailors were to be protected. The conclusion of new alliances was a wise and prudent step; other steps taken by Manuel were neither wise nor prudent. The islands had hitherto maintained their own fleets for the suppression of Saracenic pirates. The emperor ordered the money hitherto raised for this purpose to be paid into the imperial treasury, and undertook the maintenance of the fleet himself. When he had got the money, he allowed the ships to rot in harbour. Not content with ruining his navy, he proceeded to abandon the central system of army administration, by means of which his father had rendered the military force of the Eastern empire the strongest in the world. He distributed his troops in cities and provinces far apart, where they lost their discipline and their confidence. We need not attempt to follow this prince through a career full of strange vicissitudes. He fought with Raymond of Antioch, with Roger of Sicily, with the Venetians, with the Slavonian princes of Servia and Dalmatia, and with the Hungarians. He joined King Amaury of Jerusalem in his mad project to realise a Christian caliphate in Cairo. He was totally and shamefully defeated by the Turks at Myriokephalon, near Laodicea.

The great defect of his reign is that to which all despots and monarchies are especially liable. It was impossible for him personally to superintend everything. His servants were corrupt; the prodigality of his court, which he did not create, but inherited, was far beyond the resources of the empire; and Manuel was unable to see that by immediate and sweeping reforms alone could this great unwieldy structure, already tottering, be saved from falling.

Manuel's son, Alexius II., was only thirteen years of age when his father died. For the first two years of his reign the court was troubled by the perpetual intrigues of the cousins and relations of the emperor for the post of protosebastos. Nor were the intrigues confined only to the court. Factions were formed, and faction fights in the streets of the city brought with them their usual train of plunder and outrage. Looking about for a strong man, the Greeks could find no one but Andronicus, whom they invited to become prime minister, and who speedily made himself emperor.

The life of Andronicus has been drawn by every writer who has treated of the Eastern empire. In the whole of history there is no more romantic story of adventure, daring, danger, ambition, and strength. No Norman conqueror, no crusading hero, no Spanish invader, can show a more astonishing record. It may be found detailed at length in Finlay, Gibbon, and Le Beau. An abridgment of his story may be given here. He was the son of Isaac Comnenus, and the grandson of Alexius I. Like most of his race, he was tall, strong, and athletic; his personal habits were temperate; he was dexterous in arms; he was persuasive and eloquent; he owned no restraint of principle, though he was ready with quotations on occasion from St. Paul; his bravery and skill recommended him to Manuel, his cousin, whose vices as well as his courage Andronicus shared. While the emperor scandalised the Church by his connection with Theodora, his niece, Andronicus openly carried about with him Eudocia, her sister. She shared his campaigns, and the hard fighting of the day was followed by feasting and singing at night. Early in Manuel's reign Andronicus was taken prisoner by the Turks, and taken to the court of Sultan Massoud, where he learned the Turkish language, and showed no unwillingness to cast in his lot with his captors. His brother, indeed, who had become a Mohammedan, was already at the court.

On his return he was twice entrusted with the command of the army in Cilicia, and twice defeated. Subsequently he was appointed governor of the two principal fortresses on the Hungarian frontier, and again he brought disaster upon the empire. Then Manuel ceased to employ him. He returned to Constantinople, and lived aloof from the court, with Eudocia, and a crowd of actresses and dancing-girls. After a time he was suspected of a treasonable correspondence with the sultan of Iconium and the king of Hungary. There can be small doubt that he had read the annals of his country, and knew that an emperor might be dethroned. But this emperor was too strong. He might, however, be assassinated. Andronicus presented himself at an imperial hunting party, uninvited, with a numerous train of armed followers. The emperor's escort was too strong for open violence; but he was watched, and during the night Andronicus was found lurking near the emperor's tent, disguised as a Latin soldier, and armed with a dagger.

He was thrown into prison, where he remained in solitary confinement for nine years. At the end of this time he discovered some secret recess in the tower, the entrance to which he found means to close after he himself should be within it, so that it could not be suspected. Then he saved up provisions, got into his cell, and shut himself in. The prisoner had escaped. There was no apparent way out of the tower; the guards had seen no one escaping; it was impossible to find any trace of him in the neighbourhood. But he was gone. They suspected everybody, his wife among them, and they carried their suspicion so far as to lock her up in what had been her husband's cell. This was not exactly what Andronicus wanted. Probably he looked for a relaxation of the guard, or their withdrawal, now that the bird had escaped. However, things might have been worse. There was now no chance of starving, at least. In the night his wife was awakened by the spectre, as she thought, of her husband. He told her all, and after a short period, during which she managed to save food for him, the guard became neglectful, and an opportunity was found for escape.

He was caught, however, and again taken to prison, where he was loaded with chains. A second time he escaped, being able to get a model of the keys in wax, and being provided by his son Manuel with a coil of rope and new keys, conveyed to him in an amphora of wine. Again he was caught, and again by a dexterous pretence he managed to escape. This time he found himself at the court of Yaroslef, prince of Russian Galicia. Manuel was persuaded to grant him a full pardon, and he returned to the capital. He was again entrusted with the chief command in Cilicia, and he disgraced himself by another defeat. After this he thought it prudent to seek refuge in Antioch, where Raymond received him, and where he fell in love with Philippa, sister of the empress Maria. One supposes that his first wife was dead, because Philippa consented to marry him. He would not remain long in Antioch, however, lest Manuel should order his arrest. He fled to Jerusalem, and finding shelter there, showed his gratitude by falling in love with Theodora, the widow of Baldwin III., who returned his passion with equal ardour. She was thus the third princess who fell a victim to this Byzantine Don Giovanni. And when Manuel offered large rewards to any Syrian noble who should arrest Andronicus and put out his eyes, it was Theodora who warned him of the danger, and consented to take refuge with him among the Turks. A very curious chapter might be written on the renegades of the Eastern empire as well as on those of Spain. The Mohammedan service, indeed, has always attracted a certain class of adventurer. Its prizes, great and splendid, have always been open to the ready eye, the strong hand, and the quick brain; its religion is tolerant in practice if not in theory; its customs offer an apparent freedom from those bonds of morality which fetter and fatigue the piratic mind. As for Andronicus, he came of a family of renegades. With Theodora he wandered about for a time in Mesopotamia and Iberia, till he had collected a small army of refugees and Turkish mercenaries, with which, because every free and independent soldier must have money, he began to harass the frontier and capture live stock among the Christians for the slave market. He held strong forts among the mountains, to which he would retire one after the other, eluding pursuit like another Rob Roy. Nor was it until Theodora was taken prisoner that he opened negotiations with the emperor. He succeeded in gaining permission to be brought before him. Probably the permission contained a promise of freedom and forgiveness. This act was the greatest of all Manuel's mistakes. It should have been war to the knife with one so desperate and so dangerous.

Andronicus was an excellent actor. On being brought before the emperor he opened his cloak, and showed a heavy iron chain fastened to a collar round his neck. He burst into tears, quoted Scripture, and implored the pardon of his offended emperor. The pardon was promised, but that was not enough. He insisted that some one should drag him by the neck to the emperor's footstool. This kind action was performed for him by his cousin Isaac Angelus. Afterwards, when Isaac mounted the throne, the thing was remembered.

We have seen that he was chosen protosebastos. We have already stated that he murdered Alexius II. and made himself emperor. That was to be expected.

Once on the throne, the monster showed his real character again. He murdered some among the aristocracy for their wealth and influence, and put out the eyes of others—those who had helped him to his throne. Some who revolted, he punished with the greatest cruelties; and even while he made a bid for popularity by lightening the burden of taxation, he became hateful by neglecting and diminishing the public amusements.

Hated on all sides, the old man, now seventy years of age, began to be tormented by fears and anxieties. The astrologers told him that he would lose his kingdom by a man whose name began with the letter I, so that when one Isaac, who assumed the name of Comnenus, revolted and took possession of Cyprus, he thought of the prediction and awaited the end.

It was not, however, that Isaac who was to accomplish the prophecy. Among the kinsfolk of the imperial dynasty was one Isaac Angelus, a weak, harmless, and incapable man, who had hitherto excited no suspicion. It was determined, however, to arrest him, though the emperor had so low an opinion of his capacity that he refused to sign the order. The minister Agiochristophorites undertook the responsibility, and went in person to make the arrest. When Isaac heard that he was in the court of the palace, his natural cowardice turned to the fury of despair; he rushed upon the minister with his drawn sword, slew him on the spot, and sought sanctuary in the Church of St. Sophia. There his friends joined him; hither the people flocked with cries, and against his will Isaac found himself crowned.

Andronicus tried to escape, but they caught him and brought him back to the city, and before the new emperor. One loses pity for the subsequent misfortunes of Isaac when we read how he ordered one eye to be put out, one hand to be struck off, thrust him into a dungeon without food or attendance, and finally abandoned him to the brutalities of the people, who for two days subjected him to tortures which may be read in the contemporary histories, but are best not set forth in detail. For two days the wretched man thus expiated his sins, bearing his torments with fortitude, and only groaning at intervals, "Bruise not a broken reed." At last two

Latin soldiers, more humane than the Greeks, drove their swords into his heart, and ended the long life of a man who was the most remarkable outcome of the time; such a man as is only produced when the greatest courage and the finest physique belong to one who has ambition, want of principle, and strength of will, and when that man is born, like Andronicus, in a time of universal and profound corruption.

The downward course of the empire was not likely to be arrested by the accession of such a man as Isaac Angelus. Amid the anarchy, the confusion, the bribery, the impotent rage of the people, which lasted during the ten years of his feeble rule, the Vallachians established themselves on an independent footing in Thessaly. The general sent to defeat them was driven back, and in despair of conquering the barbarians, himself assumed the title of emperor and laid siege to the capital. Isaac and the city were saved by the accidental presence of Conrad of Montferrat. He told the emperor that priests and processions were very well in proper time and place, but that the present emergency demanded men; and putting himself at the head of two hundred and fifty valiant knights, with five hundred veterans, and such other forces as could be raised, he took the field and defeated the rebels. The victory brought very little benefit to the people of Constantinople, because the troops took advantage of the general rejoicing to pillage the town. Isaac was deposed, and his eyes put out by his elder brother Alexius. His son, afterwards Alexius IV., escaped.

Except that he was more treacherous, Alexius III. proved no better than Isaac II. His wife Euphrosyne conducted the business of the administration, if the sale of places, the receiving of bribes, and the farming of revenues on ruinous terms, can be called by that name. Thrace was left in the hands of the Vallachians; the admiral of the fleet sold without concealment the stores of the navy; the seas were crowded with pirates; even the emperor condescended to become a pirate, and sent six vessels into the Euxine, with private instructions to pick up what they could. Rich men were seized by parties of courtiers, and held captive until they had paid ransom. The patriarch refused to interfere; at last the people assembled before his palace and threatened to throw him out of the windows; the Venetians and Pisans fought battles in the streets; the Turks were shamefully bought off; the Bulgarians and Sclavonians were in arms; and the empire, despite the splendour and magnificence of the court, seemed on the point of falling to pieces.

The conquest of Constantinople by the Flemings and Venetians finished at a blow what the bad rule of the Comnenans was destroying rapidly and surely.

CHAPTER VIII.

THE CITY AND ITS PEOPLE.

TO those who read in history of the murders, mutilations, and depositions of emperors in quick succession, it would seem as if any man destined to be emperor at Constantinople might write himself beforehand the most wretched. But the position was so splendid, the power so boundless, that there never was wanting an ambitious man, when the chance came, ready to stake his life on a single effort—he never had more than one chance—to get the crown, and having won, to wear it, in spite of all risks and anxieties. Once on the throne, indeed, a man would easily persuade himself that he was in perfect safety, notwithstanding history and all its warnings. The acclamations of a mob might mean nothing, except to a weak and vain prince. The solid strength of the crown, however, lay, or seemed to lie, on a stronger basis than mob favour. There was the fidelity of the Imperial Guard, composed as it was, not of fickle Greeks, but of Englishmen and Danes, a stalwart and loyal troop; there was the strength of the imperial palace, which was like a fortress; there were the walls, and the strong position of the city; there was the unwarlike character of the citizens, which rendered a civic tumult rare and easily repressed; there was every day present a swarm of courtiers eager to profess loyalty; there were the vast revenues, which enabled a prodigal emperor to purchase the fidelity of thousands; and there was that unbounded magnificence of the court, which because it was so splendid seemed so safe from danger. Perhaps, too, the thoughts of the despot would turn with satisfaction to the vast armies which in Europe and Asia guarded his frontiers. These constituted, it is true, his chief danger. When an emperor failed in war, when the soldiers of Europe or Asia conceived a prejudice against his orthodoxy, his parsimony, or his weakness, there were plenty of precedents for the proclamation of their own general as emperor, and for a march, quite likely to be successful, on the capital.

First, as to the revenue of the empire. So great was it, that Theodora saved for her son the sum of 109,000 pounds weight of gold, and 300,000 pounds weight of silver; while Basil II., who maintained and paid enormous armies, accumulated no less than 200,000 pounds of gold. And Benjamin of Tudela declares that Constantinople alone brought in a revenue derived from custom duties of 20,000 pieces of gold every day. It must be remembered that everything went directly into the imperial treasury, that from every province, every city of the empire, a perennial rivulet of gold and silver flowed into those rapacious coffers; and though this revenue did not increase, as in a prosperous empire it should have done, though the powers of destruction were greater than those of recovery, yet it did not for many centuries sensibly decrease. The people who occupied the provinces of Basil or Alexius were widely different from those who held them under Constantine; but they still were subjects of the emperor, and paid him tribute. Bulgarians, Slavonians, Russians, occupied the provinces of the Greek; but the lands were tilled, and the revenue maintained.

As for the imperial palace, it was a miracle of splendour. Situated between the hippodrome, the church of St. Sophia, and the gardens, it gradually grew in extent and magnificence during eleven centuries. Every emperor who was a builder, added something or replaced something to show his taste; the long suite of chambers was decorated with paintings, statues, and mosaics of precious stones and marbles. The palace contained five churches; it was crowned with three domes, the roof, of gilt brass, rested on pillars of Italian marble, and the walls were encrusted with marbles of different colours. The costumes of those who walked in the courts and corridors were as splendid and as various as the rooms themselves of the palace. The emperor himself wore a tiara like that of the Persians, consisting of a high cap of cloth or silk covered with a profusion of pearls and jewels. The cap itself was within a horizontal circle of gold, over which rose two vertical arches: at the summit was a cross or globe, and two lappets of pearl hung down at either side. He was distinguished by purple buskins, the outward sign of rank. The costume, or rather the privileges in costume of those who stood next to him, were carefully regulated. The officers of the court, as well as the private citizens, vied with each other in magnificence of dress. Embroidery, silk, cloth of gold, entered largely into their adornment. We read of maces, battle-axes, and spears, which were gilded or covered with silver. There were gilded helmets, gilded armour, horses covered with trappings of gold and silver. There were artificial trees, with leaves of gold and jewelled automatic birds. There were purple canopies, golden thrones, everything in gold, silver, or rich silken stuff. No Oriental court, no Peruvian court, no court, modern or ancient, ever reached the splendour of Constantinople.

The emperor was, besides, encompassed with court ceremonials of a minute and tedious kind, which can now be paralleled only at St. Petersburg. The theory was, of course, to make difficulty of access heighten the idea of his grandeur. Between him and the court stood, first, the Cæsar, then the Sebastos, in later years, the Sebastocrator, the Panhypersebastos, and the Protosebastos. Then came the chief officers of the state, the Curopalata, the Protovestiaire, the Logothete, the Dragoman, the Great Domestic, the Protostrator, the Stratopedarch, the Great Duke, the Constable, the Acolyth, and the Emir, who were accommodated in palaces belonging to the emperor. But all, whether officers or plain civilians, had to approach the emperor in adoration, falling prostrate on the ground and kissing his feet. When the sovereign rode through the streets they were first cleared and purified; heralds went before, and proclaimed his coming; the people strewed flowers; every house on the line of march was hung with its most costly draperies; the factions, now no longer anxious for each other's blood, sang responsive chants on either side of the street in praise of the emperor; at the church doors he was solemnly received by the patriarch and the clergy.

As for Constantinople itself, it was in the tenth century a city which struck with astonishment the Westerns, who were accustomed to the narrow and dark streets of Paris or the winding lanes of London. There were wide open spaces, or *places*, stately churches, with ornate services, long crowded quays, splendid houses of the nobles, and a vast imperial palace. A population exceeding that of any dozen cities of France taken together, swarmed in the streets within the city and overflowed into the suburbs. They were of every nationality and wore every dress. The tall thin Copt from Egypt, the Venetian merchant with purse and inkhorn, the Pisan his rival, the Greek sailor from the islands, the mountaineer of Albania, the uncouth Russian, the stalwart Varangian guardsman, the Persian, the Armenian, the Moslem, the strange wild soldier enlisted in the Armenian highlands, and perhaps destined one day, should fortune prove evil, to seize the empire for himself, the almond-eyed Syrian, whom some, scowling, declared to be a Jew, or even, as some whispered, a Samaritan—all were there on business or for pleasure. And then there were thousands of *lazzaroni*, creatures born in the streets, living in the streets, and dying in the streets, whose daily bread was the imperial dole, whose whole business in life was to watch the criminals being scourged, blinded, deprived of tongue, hand, nose, or foot, beheaded, and hanged; to bawl at the circus, to gaze upon the processions of state, to kiss the holy pictures, and to kneel before the holy images. In times of ardent controversy, too, they discussed theology. Then there were the great palaces of the nobles—later on Venice and Pisa could show their own — and the monasteries and the multitudinous churches, each with its holy pictures, its images, and its precious relics. In the port the navy of the empire was reckoned by hundreds of war-ships, and there were the countless masts of the vessels which came and went laden with the trade of East and West. As for a middle class, that gradually disappeared. What contributed mainly to its decay was the destruction of the organized civil service. When everything began to be given to favourites, when the favourites filled up the subordinate posts with their *protégés*, the organization of the civil departments was destroyed, and with it one important element of the middle class. Then again the connection of the citizens with the army was altogether cut off by religious fanaticism. When one of the emperors asked the patriarch to declare that those who died in the frontier wars, died in a holy cause, this patriot replied that, so far from making any such declaration, he would exclude from the sacraments of the Church for three years every man who had chosen the life of a soldier. With such teaching from the churches, it cannot be a matter of surprise that the citizens learned to look on the profession of arms with contempt. Here was another outlet for a middle class destroyed.

Other causes were the accumulation of private property, which made the aristocracy rich out of all proportion, the transference of trade to foreign merchants, the intermittent successes and defeats of the empire, which were naturally felt first by the middle class, and the growth of a servile spirit among a poor and lazy population. The great families were, it is true, presently ruined, but the mischief was by this time done, and the Greek natives of the city were plunged into the lowest depths.

Yet there were always among them artificers more skilful, engineers more ingenious, scholars more learned, artists more dexterous, than in any other country of the world. Constantinople, even in its lowest stage of decay, was far in advance of the west of Europe.

The Church decayed with the people—perhaps more rapidly. It is difficult to believe that there was a vital force left at all in this great branch of the Christian Church, and it seems indeed to have become eight hundred years ago what it seems to be now—a Church of the merest formalism. There were endless ceremonies, fasts, feasts, services, worship of saints, relics, and images : to conform to all these was to ensure heaven. There were monasteries in plenty, into which it was the fashion of the aged—Isaac Comnenus retired into one—to retreat, there to pass the remainder of their days in repose and meditation. These monasteries got endowments; the endowments grew to be used for the support of the cadets of noble families in luxury. Even private houses, with all their inmates, were turned into monasteries. We have seen how many emperors, generals, and rebels were sent to repent in monastic cloisters. The church ritual was very splendid; patriarchs, bishops, and clergy vied with each other in producing the most magnificent musical services.

Such, very briefly sketched, was the Constantinople of the tenth, eleventh, and twelfth centuries. An emperor first, made sacred by every form of ceremony and state; the emperor's immediate connections, dignified by grand names, but possessing no power and having no control over affairs except that gained by personal influence; the chief officers of the state, mere private secretaries appointed at will; the strongest emperors baffled by their inability to compass the control over everything; no trained body of departmental servants; an army composed entirely of rustics and foreigners; generals suspected after every successful enterprize; a capital crowded with an unwarlike and cowardly mob, living on imperial doles, eager for the games of the circus, without interest or care for the state; and a splendid city, the most splendid city of the earth, abounding with treasures of every kind, and occupying the finest site that the world has to show.

CHAPTER IX.

THE LATIN CONQUEST.

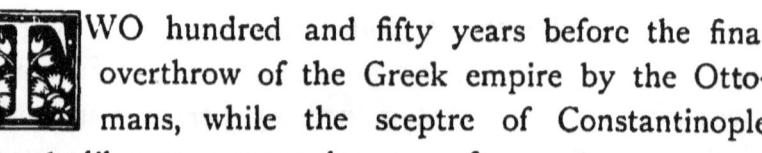TWO hundred and fifty years before the final overthrow of the Greek empire by the Ottomans, while the sceptre of Constantinople passed, like an unmeaning toy, from one grasp to another, each so feeble that the Bulgarians openly prayed that the life of him, their enemy, might be prolonged, there occurred in the dramatic history of this city an event more dramatic than anything in the records of humanity, the Latin conquest, a story before which the expedition of Pizarro pales, and the glory of Hernando Cortes is dimmed.

The horror and shame which the loss of Jerusalem spread through the whole of Christendom naturally raised up preacher after preacher, prophet after prophet, until the reverberation of the news slowly died away from shore to shore. All of them called upon princes and people to avenge the blood of the saints of Hattin, to recover the Holy Sites, to assume the Cross. None of them achieved any success until, some ten years after the city fell, Fulke de Neuilly, who possessed that divine gift which made illiterate Peter eloquent, and scholarly Bernard persuasive, began to move the laggard hearts of men and to turn them in the direction of the Holy Land. The usual signs which may be predicted of all great preachers followed in the track of his harangues. They are familiar to us now as then. There was the transitory religious revival; sinners confessed and renounced their sin, while the influence and terror of the voice was upon them; yet after a brief space the wickedness of the world went on as usual; foolish women renounced their folly, burnt their ribbons, gave up their golden bracelets, while the preacher was among them; oppressors repented their oppressions, until the preacher was gone. Fulke began, indeed, as a preacher of repentance, and it was at the instance of the newly-enthroned Pope Innocent III. that he passed—a bold and confident step for a preacher to take—from general admonition to special exhortation, and invited the young and able-bodied to wear the cross and carry a pike to Palestine.

It was not a propitious time for preaching Crusades. The kings of France and England had already fulfilled their promises, and done enough for the Cross which they had taken. To fight once on that burning soil of Syria was surely a sufficient merit for any Christian, however sinful. As well expect a Mohammedan Haj to journey on foot the whole way from Bosnia to Mecca twice in his lifetime. The Emperor of Germany was a child of six years old, and the preacher had to rely upon the leadership of those secondary princes who saw in a Crusade the opportunity of striking a blow at once for heaven and themselves. Those sovereigns who had everything to lose and nothing to gain, preferred to stay at home. What principality in the East was worth anything to Richard Lion Heart, compared with his own fair realm of England? What successes in Palestine would compensate Philip Augustus for dangers and losses at home? But to the princes who were of royal lineage, and yet of the second, third, or fourth order, a Crusade offered noble chances. Godfrey, Baldwin, Jocelyn, Tancred, Bohemon, all the princes of the first Crusade, who became kings of Jerusalem, princes, counts, dukes, and marquises of Edessa, Tripoli, Antioch, and Tyre, had been of the same rank as themselves. Glory and greatness, as well as religion, pointed in the direction of the East. Therefore it was not surprising to hear that Fulke de Neuilly, with his band of preachers, speedily roused up the Western nobles to an enthusiasm which was respectable, although, compared with that which sent forth Peter with his myriads, it was the glory of Nehemiah's Temple compared with that which the oldest men remembered with tears of the Temple which had passed away. Not twice in the world's history does the same enthusiasm seize the hearts of men.

The first chief of the fourth Crusade was Thibaut III., Count of Champagne, father of the *roi chansonnier*, Thibaut IV., poet, and platonic lover of the saintly Blanche. He was a young man of twenty-three when he placed himself at the head of the new Crusade. With him were Simon de Montfort; Baldwin, Count of Flanders, who had married a sister of Thibaut; Henry of

Flanders, brother of Baldwin; the Counts of Blois and St. Pol; Geoffrey, Count de Perche; Boniface, Marquis of Montferrat; and Geoffrey de Villehardouin, who was to be the chronicler of the adventure.

The chiefs began by sending deputies to ask the Venetians what they would charge for taking them across the water. This was business-like and prudent. They profited by the lessons of the past. They would have none of that long and toilsome march through Europe, and that unequal contest with Greek chicanery; they would avoid the perilous journey across the sands and deserts, through the marshes, and over the passes of Asia Minor, exposed to the perils of pestilence, the torments of thirst, the daily harassing of the innumerable Saracenic cavalry. Their best and safest route would be to march over the rich plains of Italy to Venice, then to take ship, and so, if the saints sent good weather, straight to the shores of the Holy Land. It will be remembered that Richard of England started with a like sensible resolve. His mistake was in being diverted from his purpose by the temptation of Cyprus; that of his successors would be the temptation of Constantinople.

It was the boast of Venice in the days of her splendour that she had never owned the yoke of any master from the days when her people fled from Attila and established themselves on their chain of low-lying islands. It was not a claim which bears the test of historical inquiry. Venice formed at one time part of the Greek empire; nor was it till Constantinople grew weak, and the city of the Adriatic strong, that she was able to throw off, little by little, the bonds which connected her with Byzantium. At this time she was stronger than before or after, though not so rich as she was destined to become. She had almost a monopoly of the great Eastern trade; she commanded an enormous fleet; she kept up commercial relations with Constantinople; she had never acquired the slavish deference to the popes which characterized the Western nations; and her government, absolutely unique, partook in no degree of the feudal system of the West or the despotism of the East. In all her transactions she studiously regarded her own interests and nothing else. She let the ambitious and aggressive Westerns struggle for the sovereignty, content if she could establish her trading stations in safety. She regarded with a sort of contempt the blind enthusiasm of French and English for holy cities, in which she only saw so many emporiums and dépôts for her wares.

At this time their Doge was the great Henry Dandolo, who is said to have been a hundred years of age at the time of his death, five years later, in 1205. We need not accept this statement as literally true. It is, however, beyond a doubt that he was extremely old, and possessed of extraordinary vigour. Thirty years before he had been deprived of sight by the Emperor Manuel Comnenus. A misfortune which would have deprived most men of desire to take any further part in politics only stimulated his ambition. He learned to see with others' eyes, and to fight with others' hands. In A.D. 1192 he was elected Doge, having then been blind for twenty years, and being, if we believe his biographers, already close upon ninety years of age. It devolved upon him, therefore, to receive the six ambassadors of the Crusaders. But he had no power to do more than listen to their proposals, entertain them hospitably, and refer them first to the Council of Six, then to the Forty composing the Council of State, and lastly to the legislative assembly of Four hundred and fifty, who were annually chosen in the six quarters of the city. What the Crusaders asked was that they might be allowed to assemble at Venice on the Feast of St. John in the ensuing year; that the Republic should find vessels for the conveyance of 4,500 horses, 9,000 squires, 4,500 knights, and 20,000 foot; that this army should be found in provisions and stores for the period of nine months; that they should be transported in Venetian ships to whatever shore the service of God and Christendom might require; and that the Republic should join them with fifty galleys.

Having announced their request, Villehardouin, who acted as speaker, summed up by declaring that they had received from the barons of France the order to entreat of the Venetians their succour in the enterprise of avenging the tomb of the Saviour, to cast themselves at the feet of the Doge, and not to rise until they had obtained a favourable answer, and the Venetians had taken pity on the Holy Land *outre mer*. Thereupon the deputies, as they had been enjoined, fell upon their knees before Dandolo, with tears in their eyes and outstretched hands. And all the assembly with one accord cried out, "We grant the prayer! We grant the prayer!"

They did grant the prayer, but with conditions; and these were hard. The Crusaders were to pay, before their embarkation, the sum of 85,000 silver marks, and all conquests were to be equally divided between Crusaders and Venetians.

The generosity or the selfishness of these terms depends entirely on the purchasing power of a silver mark. To provision 33,500 men and 4,500 horses for nine months would at the present time cost, at the low estimate of two shillings a day for each man, one million pounds sterling. To this must be added the cost of the transports and sailors—an item impossible to estimate. If we reckon a million and a half for the cost of the whole, we find that, supposing the 85,000 marks barely paid the cost, each mark had a purchasing power very nearly equivalent to that of £18 of our money. But we may be very certain that this republic of traders were not going to let slip so good an opportunity of profit.

It was more difficult to promise than to execute the treaty. The deputation returned to France after a fruitless effort to enlist the sympathies of Nice and Genoa. Their engagements were ratified by the princes. But here an unforeseen accident threatened the enterprise at its very commencement. Thibaut, Count of Champagne, the chief of the Crusade, died, and the warriors found themselves without a leader. A council was held at Soissons, where Boniface, the Marquis de Montferrat, a soldier conspicuous for gallantry and descended of a race of soldiers, was chosen to lead the Crusade. With him were the Counts of Flanders, Blois, St. Pol, and a splendid following of the greatest nobles of France and Germany.

The Crusaders arrived at Venice in the summer of 1202. Everything was ready for their departure; a splendid fleet awaited them, with abundant stores of provisions and forage; and then the awkward discovery was made that between them all the knights were not able to muster up the price agreed upon for the transport service. The reason of this unforeseen deficiency was that a great number of Flemings, French, and Italians had started by routes more convenient to themselves, and without consulting the leaders. These independent reinforcements were now awaiting the main body in the Holy Land. What was to be done? They were 34,000 marks short of the stipulated sum. Then the Doge, taking what was to be had, made a proposal. He said that the Venetians were well able to wait for the sum due until the Crusaders saw their way to discharge the debt; but in order not to delay the knights in the fulfilment of their vows, the State was ready to accept some substantial and adequate conquest by the Crusaders in full payment; that across the Adriatic was a turbulent and troublesome city named Zara, which had renounced the Venetian yoke. Let the Crusaders restore Zara to the Venetian republic, and they might then proceed together to the recovery of the Holy Land. The knights, not being able to see their way otherwise out of this difficulty, consented to do the Republic this service.

Zara was consequently taken. In other words, the *croisés*, banded together for battle against the infidel, began by fighting against Christians, and even against brother Crusaders, because Zara had thrown herself under the protection of the King of Hungary. This was a bad beginning. The pope excommunicated them all—a measure which was doubtless deplored by the Western knights, who, however, did not allow their grief to influence any of their subsequent proceedings. The Venetians, as one result of their long connection with Constantinople, were never thoroughly convinced of the supremacy of pope over patriarch, and to them excommunication meant simply unjustifiable interference with temporal matters. Therefore things went their own way, in spite of the pope.

At this juncture young Alexis, son of the captive Isaac, appeared in the camp.

We have already told his story. He was connected by marriage with the Marquis of Montferrat, whose two brothers, Reignier and Conrad, had married princesses of the Comnenan house. It was to him therefore that the young prince first opened the business. Constantinople was in the hands of a usurper; his own father, deprived of sight, was languishing in a dungeon; the people were longing to witness the dethronement of the tyrant. Was it not a worthy object of a Christian army to assist in freeing a great people? Further, could it not be made to appear worthy of a crusading army? For generations the world had been scandalized by the spectacle of a divided Christendom: that scandal should exist no longer. Surely the pope, who had excommunicated them for taking Zara, could no longer withhold his blessing if they put him in undisputed sovereignty over the whole Christian world. Again, they wanted money for the prosecution of their Crusade: he would give them 200,000 marks—a sum equivalent, if our estimate is at all correct, to three and a half millions sterling. They wanted, or would want, men: he would maintain an army in the Holy Land, to be at their command. In a word, as a drowning man catches at a straw, so Alexis was ready to promise everything.

The offer was tempting. To conquer Constantinople, replace the rightful emperor upon the throne, achieve endless glory, acquire the immense sum of 200,000 marks, restore the integrity of the Church, and then go on their way to the recovery of the Holy Places, was surely a more splendid programme than any which had yet appealed to the enthusiasm of Crusaders. But, unfortunately, it only appealed strongly to the enthusiasm of the leaders. The soldiers were indignant, and when it was decided that the young Greek's proposal should be accepted, many deserted, and found their way home, or to the Holy Land.

There is no doubt that the policy of the Doge guided the uneducated counsels of the Crusaders. The Venetian knew better than any other what advantages might be derived from the possession of this great city. What the ignorant soldiers of the West did not suspect, he knew —that those who held Constantinople could command the trade of the East. If these bulldogs of French and Flemings succeeded in conquering the city, who but the Venetians would reap the profit? Let theirs be the glory; for the Republic, the gain.

In April, 1203, the expedition left Zara, bound on the great and perilous adventure of Constantinople. Only the Venetians knew how difficult, how hopeless, save for the disorganized state of the empire, was the task before them. The fleet consisted of 440 ships, including the transports for horses, men, and provisions. They carried 40,000 soldiers. With this army they proposed to attack a city occupying a position unique for strength, believed to possess a powerful fleet, and numbering perhaps a population of half a million. No city in the West numbered more than a tenth of that estimate.

The ignorant soldiers, sailing with a light heart to encounter these perils, met with neither bad weather nor hostile fleets, as the gallant company of galleys and transports passed down the Adriatic, across the Ægean, and up the Dardanelles. They even crossed the Sea of Marmora and passed under the very walls of the city without other peril than the discharge of darts and stones from the Greeks, who gazed at them, secure behind their walls, with more of curiosity than of terror. It was indeed only sixteen years since the unsuccessful attack of Alexis Ducas helped to make the people believe their city to be impregnable. With their line of towers and walls guarding, not only the tongue of land on which the city was built, but also the landward side, with the fortifications of Galata, the great chain barring the mouth of the Golden Horn, their Varangian guards, their innumerable soldiers, what had they to fear from this handful of Western barbarians? Nothing, had their fighting power been equal to their defensive bulwarks.

Where was their fleet? This, which ought to have met the Venetians in the narrow seas, was found reduced to twenty galleys. Only twenty galleys represented the naval power of what was proudly called the Roman empire. Malversations of the admirals, treachery, neglect, and want of confidence, had brought about this result. The paltry fleet lay hiding in the Golden Horn, useless.

The Crusaders landed at Scutari, and hither came, the next day, a deputation from Alexis, asking in haughty terms what he was to understand by this hostile demonstration, and inviting them, on pain of speedy and condign punishment, to return whence they had come. The Crusaders replied that they could not recognize him as emperor at all, that they were come to restore the rightful king to the throne; but that if he agreed to resign the crown at once, they would intercede with the injured Isaac, and gain for him at least the promise of his life. They followed up this message by transporting their cavalry across the Bosporus, and routed in very encouraging style the first Greek troops sent out against them.

It was necessary, however, to occupy, with as little delay as possible, the Golden Horn. This was protected by a great chain lying across the mouth, and secured at either end within a tower. The Venetians armed their heaviest transport with a pair of gigantic shears, and drove her against the chain. Whether by the weight of the ship or by the use of the shears, is not certain, the chain was broken, the Venetian fleet crowded into the port, and the capture of the city was now a practicable enterprise.

It might be attacked by complete investment or be taken by storm. The first was out of the question, from the small number of the besiegers. But they held command of the sea. It was resolved, therefore, that the Crusaders should concentrate their forces at the northern angle of the city wall. It was impossible to blockade the city gates, or to keep the besieged from sorties. Baldwin, Count of Flanders, led the van with the Belgian chivalry. The main body, consisting of Flemings under Henry, brother of Baldwin, and French under the Counts of Blois and St. Pol, was commanded by the Marquis of Montferrat. The engines which had been constructed for use against the walls of Jerusalem were taken from the ships and erected in position.

Mean time the Venetians were to assail the city from the ships near the centre of the line of wall protecting the shore of the Golden Horn.

As soon as a breach had been effected in the wall, a general assault by sea and land was delivered. That by land was begun with the usual desperate courage of the Crusaders, who found opposed to them, not the effeminate arms of the Greeks, but the sturdy axes of English and Danish guards and Pisan mercenaries. The assailants were repulsed in the utmost disorder. This was the chance which comes to him who knows how to use it. Had the emperor, who witnessed the contest from a window in the Blachern Palace, placed himself at the head of his Varangians, and led a sortie on the flying foe, he must have ended then and there the crusade against his empire. Had he even given permission to Theodore Lascaris, his warlike son-in-law, who was at his side in readiness, the end would have been certain. But Alexis did not move. In his sluggish veins there was no impulse possible of generous valour, even when his crown and his life were at stake.

So the opportunity was lost. When it was too late Alexis ordered his troops to march out in battle array before the walls. But they did not attack the Latins, who for their part had had for that day enough of fighting.

The Venetians, however, were on their side completely successful. They had furnished their vessels with high wooden towers provided with drawbridges, which were to be let down on the walls of the city. These vessels, filled with men, were supported by galleys whose tops were filled with archers and crossbow-men, who supported the attack and swept the defenders from the fortifications. The blind old Doge was on board, clad in complete armour, and when the signal was given he ordered his crew to press on, that he might be among the first to touch the walls. After a short struggle the bridges were lowered, and the Venetians swarmed upon the walls, beating back the defenders everywhere, until the twenty-five towers and the connecting line of wall were in their possession. It was more difficult to occupy the town by storm, as the narrow streets were easily defended. The houses were fired before them; but while the conflagration spread, and the unfortunate Greeks fled out of them for safety, the news was hastily brought that the

Crusaders were defeated, that the Byzantine army was in full array outside the walls, and that the emperor was about to attack the camp in overwhelming numbers. The Doge ordered the walls to be abandoned, and the ships with all the men-at-arms and archers to return for the support of their allies. But the Greeks were already returning to the city.

There was no occasion for another assault, because the emperor that night, whether terrified by secret information of treachery, which is very possible, or despairing of making a successful defence, or out of sheer cowardice, collected together what he could carry of jewels and money, and with a few of his friends fled from Constantinople. It was at the dawn of day that his flight was discovered. In the confusion which ensued, one Constantine, a eunuch, succeeded in persuading the Varangian guard to replace Isaac II. on the throne. The blind prisoner was awakened in the monastery where he had been confined, by the armed tramp of those who were taking him from a dungeon to a throne. It was the second great dramatic event in the life of this undeserving *fainéant*.

He was proclaimed emperor, with his son, Alexis IV., as colleague. The Crusaders were disappointed. What they longed to effect by arms and courage, had been done for them by the feebleness of the usurper. There was, therefore, to be no sack of this rich and prosperous city. The Venetians, more wary, suspected some kind of treachery. They resolved on keeping young Alexis as a hostage, while they sent an embassy to Isaac, acquainting him with the treaty made by his son, and asking him if he intended to carry out the terms. The emperor declared his willingness to ratify the treaty so far as promises were concerned, but he confessed that he saw no probability of keeping his promise. What Dandolo wanted, however, was the promise. It would be his business, later on, to remind the emperor of his engagements.

The promise given, a grand triumphant entry was made into Constantinople, the young emperor riding between Dandolo and Count Baldwin.

There was no enthusiasm among the people at the return of the blind old monarch; there was so little national spirit left among them, that they conceived no hope of future improvement in the gallant young prince who rode between the Doge of Venice and the Count of Flanders. They despaired of better things; they were like the Romans when one bad pope came after another bad pope, and they could hope for nothing better than new and more biting epigrams. The Greeks of Constantinople looked with hatred on their rulers, as they looked with contempt upon their priests.

The present state of things, indeed, offered small cause for congratulation to a patriotic mind. To raise the 200,000 marks promised by the prince who had brought these Western warriors upon the city, the imperial palace was stripped of plate, gold, silver, and jewels; the altars were robbed of the sacred vessels, and the holy pictures stripped of their silver frames; the monasteries were deprived of the treasures which pious men and women had stored up in them. And yet the whole did not nearly suffice.

Nor was that all. This army, which they had driven from before their walls, and which now behaved as if it had been victorious, had to be fed. Where was the money to buy provisions for them? Where were the provisions themselves to come from? For the Latins had settled their camp over the richest and most fertile suburbs of the city, where they plundered and devoured at their will.

The two emperors, father and son, who might at least have maintained the dignity of the Byzantine crown, were ridiculous and degraded in the eyes of the people. For the father, led on by the promises of astrologers and monks, who held out hopes of the recovery of his sight and the gift of a prolonged life, spent his time in entertaining these charlatans and spiritual jugglers; while the son, probably glad to escape the mortifications of the impoverished court, was always in the Crusaders' camp, feasting, gambling, singing, and drinking with the rough young knights, who treated him with no more courtesy than they showed to each other.

The situation was intolerable, and it was destined to become worse. Still there was hope. At the end of September the Crusaders would embark again and set sail, leaving Constantinople, it might be hoped, for ever. So, at least, it was arranged. What Dandolo proposed to do if the conditions of the treaty were not fulfilled, no one cared to inquire. The French and Flemish barbarians, the rough and unmannerly Western knights, with no knowledge of Homer and no respect for Byzantine titles and ceremonies, would go. That was the main thing.

But on the night of August 19, six weeks before the day fixed for the embarkation of the troops, there happened a dreadful misfortune. A party of Flemish soldiers were drinking at the house of a Flemish merchant. Being probably drunk, they conceived the idea of plundering a church close to their friend's house, and of looting certain warehouses filled with valuable stuffs from Syria and Egypt. They were not too drunk to carry this brilliant conception into immediate execution. But the people rose upon them when they had as yet scarcely commenced their exploit, and they saw that flight was here the better part of valour. They fled, the Greeks vindictively pursuing them. Whether to save themselves by a diversion, or out of revenge, these gallant fellows, whose proceedings inspire one with a lively admiration for Crusaders, set fire to the houses as they passed. Unfortunately a strong wind blew across the peninsula, and spread the conflagration so rapidly that it was impossible to arrest the flames. The fire lasted for two nights and a day. When it was finally subdued, there remained a long belt of charred and smoking relics, stretching a mile and a half in length, from the Golden Horn to the Propontis. The fire had raged through the wealthiest quarter of the city. Innumerable monuments of ancient art, numbers of precious manuscripts, boundless accumulated wealth of that kind of which Constantinople was now the only depository, perished in those flames wantonly kindled by the drunken Flemings.

One does not hear what was done to the authors of the mischief. Perhaps they were sitting on the shore of Galata, laughing over the brilliant success of their exploit. But the effects of that drinking bout were very remarkable and lasting, as will be seen. It is indeed seldom that one can follow the consequences of a crime, a vulgar, thoughtless, and brutal crime, so fully, or with such clearness.

For, first of all, when the richest part of the city had been burned down, and the stores of wealth destroyed, it was impossible for the imperial government to seek for aid among the resources of private citizens. The golden candelabra and the vessels of St. Sophia, the Byzantine mother-church, when melted down, went but a very little way. And then Alexis, this young boon companion of Flemish roysterers, was fain to seek the Latin camp and confess that he could not pay the money.

Dandolo was not displeased. So far as things had gone, it seemed possible that Venice would get no good at all out of this costly and dangerous business. He said that they were in no immediate hurry. They would wait the convenience of their imperial hosts. They would stay where they were for six months longer. In six months, surely, the money could be raised. Mean time the Greeks would have the pleasure of finding provisions for the Latin and Venetian armies, which, for their part, would continue to keep their camps on the more desirable and fertile portions of the *campagna*, so that neither revenue nor harvests could be looked to from that quarter. Also, their soldiers should continue to pay friendly visits to their countrymen in the city, and it was to be hoped that no more fires would be the consequence. Of course the Greeks could do nothing but acquiesce, or fight, and they did not like fighting.

Three months passed in ceaseless endeavour to complete this unpopular tax of 200,000 marks. Isaac continued to feast his astrologers and lying monks, and Alexis found his sole delight in the Latin camp. The people murmured, whispered, and told stories to each other. In January, the hungry dogs of war across the Golden Horn sent a message to the two emperors. Unless the money was paid immediately, they would be compelled to declare war. One does not quite understand the policy of this announcement. The Venetians, one would think, must have known the true state of affairs—the utter poverty of the empire, the general collapse of all its resources. Perhaps they hoped by such a measure to obtain large concessions for their trading interests, to keep Pisa and Genoa out of the Dardanelles altogether, to take advantage of the weakness of Constantinople—just as, six hundred and seventy years later, the Russians would try to take advantage of the weakness of Turkey—and make that queen of cities a vassal and dependent on Venice.

They could hardly have reckoned on what really happened, which would have been too much of a risk to face. For the people—would that contemporary historians would tell us more of the poor, suffering, patient people—refused to bear any more, and rose in swift and sudden revolt. It was the evening of January 25, 1204.

They brought together in the cathedral of St. Sophia the members of the senate, the nobles, and the clergy, and they bade them elect, there and then, a new emperor. A little respite was gained, because in that time of suspense and peril it was no easy matter to find a man courageous enough to take upon himself this dangerous distinction. Three days of anarchy and confusion followed. Isaac II., luckily for himself, seized this opportunity of dying. Then, as no one would become emperor, the mob seized on a young man, named Nicolas Kanavos, and proclaimed him emperor, against his will.

Young Alexis IV. turned with despairing eyes upon the Latin camp. There, and there alone, seemed to be his chance of safety. He made hasty and secret arrangements with the Marquis of Montferrat for the admission of the Crusaders into the city, and waited their arrival. He would have done better either to trust to his Varangian guard, or to fly to the Latin camp without delay. But these Greek emperors trusted no one, and if they fought, or if they fled, seemed always to fight or fly too late.

Late in the evening, while Alexis was expecting, perhaps, the arrival of some of his Latin defenders, he received a visit from Alexis Ducas, called, from the thickness of his beetling eyebrows, Murtzuphlos. This man was one of the officers of the household, chamberlain or keeper of the imperial wardrobe. He came into the presence of the young emperor, hurriedly, without ceremony, urging immediate flight from the rage of a maddened mob, which he represented as close at his heels. There was no mob. But the unhappy youth, begging Murtzuphlos to help him in his escape, confided to his care the imperial insignia, and entrusted himself to his guidance to be led, by devious ways, into the Crusaders' camp.

By devious ways, indeed, but not to the Latin camp. For the treacherous Murtzuphlos led him to a dungeon, into which he thrust him, and went on his way to consummate his plot.

This was, naturally, to become emperor. He was raised to that office by the acclamations of the army. The young man they called Nicolas Kanavos came down joyfully from the throne on which he never wished to be seated. Alexis IV. was strangled in his prison, and Alexis V. reigned in his stead.

It is unfortunate for Alexis the Beetle-browed that the description of his character has fallen into unfriendly hands, who represent him as a traitor, murderer, robber, and usurper. That he was all these there can be no doubt. Let us, however, concede in his favour that he was the only man of the time, until Theodore Lascaris came to the front, who could command fear, ensure order and discipline, and make himself obeyed by his craven countrymen. He was the one strong man left in the city during those disastrous days. He was valiant, as everybody knew; he was active in overlooking the execution of the works for defence; he was even to be met at night, carrying that terrible battle-axe of his, patrolling the streets, to maintain order. So far, he was an admirable prince. But he insisted on the citizens doing something for themselves. There should be no payment of others to do the fighting while he wore the purple; there should be a *levée en masse;* the merchants from their shops, the mechanics from their trades, the sturdy beggars from their sunny corners, should all alike stand up and be drilled side by side, or be sent out with pike and lance to fight the Latin foe. This made him unpopular. A man might be a murderer, a traitor, and a usurper, in that Greek empire, and yet be a favourite with the people. What was not allowed was that he should interfere with the cowardice and the supineness of the citizens. And when, to pay for his expenses, he imposed ruinous taxes, and even laid hands upon their property, his name began to be held in execration as much as his terrible face in fear.

Alexis could make them stand up and pretend to be soldiers; he could not make them fight. Once, and once only, he led them out to meet the Crusaders. With one accord they turned and fled, so that he tried that experiment no more. And now, even to him, it seemed evident that the city must fall.

Three months after the usurpation of Alexis the Crusaders resolved upon making a general and united attack. This time it would seem as if the counsel of the Venetians was followed, because the attempt on the land wall was not renewed, the whole strength of the army being hurled against the long line of wall facing the Golden Horn. This plan was advantageous to Alexis, it enabled him to place the whole of his Varangians and Pisans upon the battlements. It was advantageous to the assailants, because their own forces were not strong enough for division, as had been already proved. Moreover, the weakness of the wall lay in the fact that it possessed no flank defences; it was all curtain; and there were the quays, of which the assailants could take advantage for landing troops, scaling-ladders, and engines. The Crusaders attacked from the ships of the Venetians by means of drawbridges and wooden towers. Nevertheless, after a fight of extraordinary fury, the Latins had to retire, with the loss of many of their bravest soldiers.

Three days later, on the 12th of April, they renewed the attack, this time with better success. They had bound their ships together in pairs; they had raised the wooden bulwarks of their decks, and enlarged the tops which held the archers, so that they could bring to bear upon any point of the walls a concentrated volley of missiles. These tactics succeeded, aided by the arrows and bolts from the other ships. The two united vessels, the *Paradise* and the *Pilgrim*, laid three bridges upon one of the towers of the wall, which was instantly occupied by their men. Crowds poured in at this avenue, and within a few minutes four or five of the towers, with the wall between, were in the hands of the Crusaders. Then they opened three of the city gates, landed their horses from the ships in the rear, and prepared to take the town, street by street if necessary, by storm. But here the Varangians and the Pisans declined the contest. They refused to fight any more, and carried the emperor to his palace of Bucoleon. The Crusaders for their part seized and occupied the palace of Blachern, near the northern angle of the wall, the same palace from which Alexis watched their abortive assault, and as the day was too far gone for further work, set fire to the houses. It is said that more houses were destroyed in these successive conflagrations than were contained in any three cities of France all taken together.

The usurper had nothing left but flight. He took with him his wife Eudocia and his mother Euphrosyne, embarked in a galley, and disappeared from the city. He was destined, however, to return to it again, a prisoner, to receive the doom of death.

The city almost in the hands of the enemy, the flames raging through street after street, their emperor fled, their Varangians refusing to fight—what was to be done? The people ran shouting and crying to their great Church of St. Sophia: would any one become emperor? It showed how deeply the spirit of superstition had sunk into the Byzantine heart, that, whatever was the emergency, they always began by proclaiming an emperor. They were helpless without one; they had lost the power of independent action; they trembled at responsibility. This mental condition is the most inevitable, as it is the worst, result of imperialism.

They elected Theodore Lascaris, son-in-law of Alexis III. He undertook to rouse, if possible, the Varangians to resistance. They still refused to fight. Probably they were disgusted at the helplessness of a city of half a million which suffered itself to be taken by an army of 30,000 men. Without fighting, it was useless to remain as an emperor within the walls of the city. The elected sovereign of one night, therefore, followed his predecessor in flight, so that there were now three Greek emperors fugitives. That was one remarkable result of the Crusade. A fourth emperor had died in his bed, and a fifth had been strangled. Five emperors disposed of in six months.

Now, however, there was no more fighting. The city was in the hands of the Western Christians. They behaved as Christian soldiers, whether of the East or West, always have behaved: they pillaged, destroyed, burned, outraged, and murdered.

When there was a pause, from sheer fatigue, in a sack as full of horrors as that which three hundred years later was to fall on the sister city of Rome ; when the men-at-arms sat down and slept, weary with murder and pillage ; when before the stripped and naked altars, on which shameless women had been set to dance and sing for their amusement, lay the ribald soldiers, on whose arm was sewn in mockery the red cross ; when the Latin clergy had run from church to church, collecting at every one the holy relics with which the city abounded—the chiefs began to take thought of order. A solemn thanksgiving was held in the Church of St. Sophia. It was ordered that all the booty should be collected and brought to certain churches, where it was valued and divided according to the agreement already concluded between the Venetians and the Flemings.

It was certainly necessary that some such agreement should be arrived at. The Venetians began by demanding that the freight of the expedition should first be paid out of the plunder, a proposal which left it open to themselves to estimate the cost of this freight at their own price. This danger was averted by the concession that the Venetians should receive three-quarters of the plunder and the Latins the rest.

An immense quantity of the booty was of course stolen and withheld by soldiers, knights, and clergy. An incalculable amount of wealth had been wrecked in the conflagrations, and stores of precious things whose value was unknown to these rude warriors — manuscripts, statues, works of art—had been ruthlessly destroyed by the conquerors.

Gibbon borrows from Nicetas a list of the principal statues which were overthrown and destroyed. Many of these were of bronze or brass, and were melted down, not for the sake of wanton mischief, but for the value of the metal.

Still there remained a goodly pile of precious things. The value of the booty was estimated at 300,000 marks of silver, each mark being equal to a pound weight. The Crusaders paid up their debt to the Venetians, and were able, dividing the remainder of their portion into shares represented in the proportion of 1 : 2 : 4, to give to foot-soldiers, horsemen, and knights, respectively the sum of three, six, and twelve marks. If, as was roughly calculated above, the purchasing power of each mark was equal to that of £18 of our own money, it will be seen that the capture of Constantinople was a fairly good day's work; but of course nothing to what under more economical management and without three fires it ought to have been, and no doubt was expected to have been. One wonders how much of this money ever reached Western Europe.

As for the people, the sacking and the plunder once over, they went on with their usual work. The misfortunes of the city fell chiefly on the rich; there was some comfort in witnessing the impoverishment of those who had fattened on their leanness. They were always poor; their poverty was not likely to be much worse under the Latins than it had been under their own chiefs; if a man has nothing he can lose nothing. Nor was their indignation at the insults offered to their religion much greater than their indignation at the national disgraces. These insults affected the clergy, and between clergy and people a great gulf had gradually grown up, widening year by year.

The conquest of Constantinople meant nothing less than the overthrow of the old Roman Empire of the East; for although the Latins remained in possession for no more than sixty years, when the Greeks came back, the old things were either gone, or survived but as a shadow of what they had been. There comes a time in the history of old monarchies when things which are but shadows, such as court ceremonies, court titles, court dignities, seem like things real and substantial; but when they go they can never be revived. A shadow may seem to be real, seen in certain lights; but when its shadowy character has been apprehended, it can never again, in any light, appear to be what it is not. All the antiquated forms, the empty ceremonials, which had surrounded the throne of Byzantium for nine hundred years, were swept away. The tenures of the land were changed. Old notions of law, justice, religion, social customs, rank, were changed suddenly. When the last Courtenay emperor fled, as Alexis III., Alexis V., and Theodore Lascaris fled, in secret and by night, his conquerors came back, as Louis XVIII. did, to a place which was strange and new to those who yet remembered the old traditions.

CHAPTER X.

THE LATIN EMPIRE.

BEFORE the final assault upon the city, Dandolo insisted upon an agreement as to the partition of the empire. It was quite understood by the Venetians, who proved in the sequel to have entirely misapprehended the resources, the strength, and the weakness of the Byzantine possessions, that he who held Constantinople held the key of the East. It was their policy not to be the holders of the key, because those who held had to defend; but to be on such terms of friendship with the holders as did not necessarily mean an alliance, so that, should a change of masters take place, the Venetians might be fettered by no troublesome bonds of obligation. Venice fought for her own hand. Other nations were continually led astray by illusory hopes of allies and friends bound by ties of gratitude. And yet even to this nineteenth century, and the middle of it, treaties have proved useless, when the interest of any signatory power was backed by strength. Nor can we wonder at the perfidy of the middle ages, when we have seen the perfidy of Russia;

we can hardly even blame the interested diplomacy of Dandolo, when we have seen ourselves, in this very year of grace, the noblest eloquence of England's greatest statesman encouraging England's most persistent and most dangerous enemy. Treaties are as the smoke of a tobacco-pipe, when strength and interest point in the same direction. By the persistent breach of sacred treaties Rome destroyed Carthage; and in modern days it seems as if national obligations may be repudiated if only a political opponent can be thwarted and embarrassed.

The Latins in command of Constantinople, it became necessary then to proceed at once to the partition of the Roman empire. It had been agreed by Dandolo on the one hand, and Baldwin, Boniface, and the Counts of Blois and St. Pol on the other, that one full quarter of the whole dominion was to be assigned to the Latin emperor, who was to be elected by Venetians and Crusaders. There remained three-quarters. Of this Venice was to have a moiety, and the rest was to be divided somehow among the Crusaders. Not a word about Jerusalem or the Holy Places. Even the acquisition of that share of the 300,000 marks which fell to each soldier failed to stimulate the Crusaders to the accomplishment of their vows.

First of all, however, they proceeded to elect an emperor.

Venice wanted no dignity of that kind, nor could any dignity be bestowed upon the nonagenarian Dandolo greater than that which he actually enjoyed as Doge of his native Republic. He accepted, however, the title of Despot of Romania. The emperor must therefore be chosen from among the French or Flemings. Two of the chiefs might show strong claims for the choice. Of these two, the Marquis of Montferrat, who at first seemed the most likely to be chosen, was already connected by means of his brother's marriage with the late reigning dynasty of Constantinople. He was, besides, proved to be a valorous soldier and a prudent general. On the other hand, Baldwin, the Count of Flanders, a younger man, had displayed all the prowess of his rival, and was personally more popular. Besides, the larger part of the army consisted of his own people, Flemings. There was therefore no surprise when the council of election announced that their choice had fallen upon Baldwin, and his rival was among the first to acknowledge the validity of the election. The Marquis of Montferrat obtained for his prize Crete and the Asiatic part of the empire. As, however, he discovered that the latter part of the Byzantine realm would require to be conquered, he exchanged it for the kingdom of Thessalonica. The Greek empire had at one blow fallen to pieces. What the Crusaders had conquered was that part of the country now called Roumelia. Across the Dardanelles, Theodore Lascaris established himself as emperor at Nicæa; an Alexis of the Comnenan House, a son of Manuel Comnenus, created an empire for himself at Trebizond; another established himself as Despot of Epirus; and the other two wandering emperors— Alexis III. and Alexis V., the Beetle-browed—joined their forces, in the hope of keeping the Latins out of the north-west provinces. But these two past masters in duplicity could not, even in misfortune, trust one another, and Alexis III., the craftier, if not the stronger of the two vagabond usurpers, seized his ally, put out his eyes, and handed him over to the Latins. They went through the formality of a trial, and found him guilty of the murder of Alexis IV. He was sentenced to death, and after a good deal of discussion it was decided that the manner of his death should be by being hurled from the top of a lofty column, and this was accordingly done.

As for Alexis III., after a great variety of adventures he finally fell into the hands of his son-in-law, Theodore Lascaris, who shut him up in a monastery, where his troubled life came to an end.

Baldwin began his reign by sending a conciliatory letter to the pope. He had not, it is true, attempted to carry out the vows which he and his brother *croisés* had taken upon themselves. Palestine still groaned under the yoke of the infidel. At the same time, the Pope could not but feel gratified at the extinction of the Greek schism and the restoration of the unity of Christendom. That event was undoubtedly due to him, and the pope acknowledged it in a careful letter, which left him free at any time to express his disapprobation of the course pursued by the Crusaders. To the king of France Baldwin wrote, inviting the French knights to find their way to this new scene of conquest and glory. To Palestine he sent promises of assistance, with, as tokens of his power, the gates of Constantinople, and the chain which barred the port.

And then, the empire being fairly parcelled out, the Marquis of Montferrat took his knights and men-at-arms to establish his own kingdom of Thessalonica. Other chiefs, who had obtained each his own part of the Byzantine territories, went off to conquer them for themselves; and the Greeks began to perceive that they were ruled by a mere handful of Latin adventurers, only to be dreaded when they were together, and now scattered in small garrisons and feeble bands all about the country. When this knowledge was thoroughly acquired, troubles began to befall the new empire.

These troubles were originated, however, not by the Greeks but by the Bulgarians, and were due to the arrogance and pride of Baldwin. John, or Kalo-John, or Joannice, as he is variously called, king of this savage people, was of the Latin Church. Being as orthodox as he was barbarous, he rejoiced mightily at the fall of the Greeks, and sent an embassy of congratulation to the new Latin emperor. Weak as he was upon his unstable throne, Baldwin actually had the folly and impudence to assault these ambassadors, to treat them as rebels, and to send a message to their master, that before his servants could be received at the Byzantine court, he must first deserve pardon by touching with his forehead the footstool of the imperial throne. It was not likely that a high-spirited and independent sovereign would brook such a message. He instantly threw the whole weight of his influence and strength into the cause of the Greeks, and with their leaders concerted a scheme of general and simultaneous massacre, worthy of his barbarism and their treachery. The secret was well kept. The conspirators were in no hurry to strike the blow. They waited patiently till a time when it seemed as if the force of the Latins was at the lowest, that is, when Prince Henry, brother of the emperor, had crossed the Hellespont with the flower of the troops. The empire in Europe was covered with thin and sparse garrisons; there were no forces in Constantinople to come to their succour should they try to hold out; they might be taken in detail and at once. And then those Byzantine Vespers began. It was a revolt of thousands against tens; there was a great slaughter, a rush of the little bands who escaped, upon Adrianople, where there was a fresh slaughter; and while the Greeks were up in successful revolt, the Bulgarians, accompanied by a savage band of 14,000 Comans, invaded the country, mad for pillage and revenge.

The position was one of extreme peril. Baldwin sent messengers to his brother, ordering him to return in all haste, and then made such hasty preparations as were possible, and sallied forth to the siege of Adrianople. Had he waited for Henry's return all might have gone well with him, but he would not wait. It was the rule of the Crusaders never to refuse battle, whatever the odds, a rule to which their greatest victories as well as their greatest disasters were chiefly due. What Godfrey did before Ascalon, Baldwin was ready to do before Adrianople. He had with him no more than a hundred and forty knights, with three trains of archers and men-at-arms—say a couple of thousand men in all. The gallant

Villehardouin, Marshal of Romania, who was destined to survive this day and write its story, led the vanguard. The main body, with whom was Baldwin, was commanded by the Count of Blois; the rear was brought up by old Dandolo. The slender ranks of the little army were continually being recruited by the accession of the fugitive remains of the garrisons. On the way to Adrianople they met the light cavalry of the Comans. Orders were given not to pursue these light horsemen, who fought after the manner of the Parthians. In a solid phalanx the Western knights were able to face any odds, but scattered and dispersed, they would fall beneath the weight of numbers.

The order insisted on by Dandolo, who knew this kind of enemy, was broken by no others than the emperor himself and the Count of Blois. The Comans, as usual, fled at the first charge of the heavily-armed knights, who spurred after them, regardless of the order, and led by the emperor. When they had ridden a mile or so, when their horses were breathed, then the Comans closed in upon the little band of knights, and the unequal contest began of a hundred and forty against fourteen thousand. Some few struggled out of the *melée* and found their way back to the rest of the army. Most fell upon the field. Among these was the Count of Blois. A few were taken prisoners, among whom was the emperor.

No one ever knew his fate. The wildest stories were told of this unfortunate prince. His hands and feet, it was said, were cut off, and he was exposed, mutilated, to the wild animals; he was beheaded; he enacted the part of

Joseph, Potiphar's wife being King John's queen. Nothing was too wild to be believed about him. Twenty years later a hermit of the Netherlands thought it would be possible to pass himself off as the real Baldwin, who had escaped from captivity, and was thus expiating his early sins. He obtained the fate from justice and the sympathy from the vulgar which have commonly been the lot of pretenders. Whatever the real end of this emperor, King John wrote a year later to the pope, calmly informing him that his intercession for Baldwin was no longer of any use, because he was no longer living. Then it was, and not till then, that his brother, Henry of Flanders, consented to assume the title of emperor.

Already the leaders of the Crusade, who only three years before had set sail so proudly from Venice, were dead or on the point of death. Baldwin murdered in captivity; the Count of Blois killed on the field of battle; Dandolo dead, at the age, say some writers, of a hundred, in the year 1205; the Marquis of Montferrat about to be slain in an obscure skirmish with the barbarous Bulgarians. Henry stood alone, save for the faithful Geoffrey de Villehardouin, Marshal of Champagne and Romania, who, though his narrative ceases at this point, is believed to have remained with the new emperor.

His reign lasted for ten years only. It was a reign of successful, brave, and prudent administration in things military, civil, and ecclesiastical. Its success was greatly assisted by the fact that very early in his reign the Greeks discovered the mistake they had made in changing the rule of the Latins for the rule of the Bulgarians.

The first were hard masters, with rough rude ways, and little sympathy with the culture of the Byzantines; but the latter proposed, as soon as the Latins were driven south, to exterminate the population of Thrace, or at least to transplant the Greeks beyond the Balkans. They called upon the emperor to forgive them, and to help them. Henry, with a little army of 800 knights, with archers and men-at-arms, perhaps 5,000 in all, made no scruple of going out to attack this disorderly mob of 40,000 Bulgarians. As no mention is made of the Comans, it is presumable that these had gone home again with their booty. At the siege of Thessalonica King John was murdered—slain by no less a person than St. Demetrius himself, said the Greeks—and a peace was concluded between his successor and Henry. The last years of this exemplary monarch's life were spent in wise administration. He checked the zeal of the pope's legate, and would not countenance persecution about the double procession and other controverted dogmas. He checked the pretensions of the clergy, by placing his throne on the same level with that of the patriarch, whereas it had formerly been lower; and he prohibited the alienation of fiefs, which would have handed over the patrimony of the knights to the Church, and turned, as Gibbon says, a colony of soldiers into a college of priests.

When he died childless, the next heir to the empire was his sister Yolande, who had married Peter of Courtenay, Count of Auxerre, a member of that princely house which still survives in the line of the English earls of Devon. It was an unfortunate day for that prince when he accepted the crown which had already in ten years carried off two of his brothers. Yet the chance was splendid. What count or duke or knight of these days but would seize a crown thus offered, however great the peril? He accepted the crown, then, and, to make a worthy appearance on entering into possession, he either mortgaged or sold the best part of ten estates, and raised, with the help of Philip Augustus, an army of 140 knights and 5,500 men-at-arms and archers. He persuaded the pope, Honorius III., to crown him, it being understood that, as emperor of the East, he had no claim to jurisdiction or right over Rome; and following the example of Baldwin, engaged the Venetians to convey him and his army to Constantinople. They would do so on similar terms and for a consideration. Let him first recover for them the port of Durazzo from the Despot of Epirus. This was no longer Michael, the founder of the kingdom, but his brother Theodore. The emperor delivered his assault on Durazzo, and was unsuccessful. Then the Venetians refused the transports. Peter thereupon made an agreement with the Despot Theodore, by which the latter undertook to convey him and his army safely to his dominion over land. It is another story of Greek treachery. The emperor with his troops, while in the mountains, was attacked by Greeks of Theodore's army. Such of his men as did not· surrender, were cut to pieces. He himself was taken prisoner, detained for two years, and then put to death in some mysterious way. Yolande, the empress, while yet she was uncertain of the fate of her lord, gave birth to a son, the most unfortunate Baldwin.[1]

The eldest of Yolande's sons, Philip de Courtenay, had the singular good sense and good fortune to decline the offered crown. He found plenty of fighting in Europe of an equally adventurous kind, and less treacherous than that among the Greeks. The second son, Robert, accepted the responsibilities and dangers of the position. For seven years he held the sceptre with a trembling hand amid all kinds of disasters. The Despot of Epirus, the treacherous Theodore, swept across the country as far as Adrianople, where he raised his standard and called himself emperor. Vatatces, the successor of Theodore Lascaris, seized upon the last relics of the Asiatic possessions, intercepted Western succour, actually persuaded a large body of French mercenaries to serve under him, constructed a fleet, and obtained the command of the Dardanelles. A personal and private outrage of the grossest kind, offered to the unfortunate emperor by an obscure knight, drove him in rage and despair from the city. He sought refuge in Italy, but was recalled by his barons, and was on his way back to Constantinople when he was seized with some malady which killed him. It is a miserable record of a weak and miserable life.

[1] The following genealogy may be useful:—

BALDWIN I.,
succeeded by his brother HENRY,
succeeded by his sister YOLANDE = PETER OF COURTENAY.

| PHILIP. | ROBERT. | BALDWIN II. |

On his death, his brother Baldwin being still a boy, the barons looked about them for a stronger hand to rule the tottering state. They found the man they wanted in gallant old John de Brienne, the last of those who raised themselves from simple knightly rank to a royal palace. The House of Brienne in France ranked next to that of Montmorency, and with that noble House was among the most illustrious of those which graced the early mediæval period. They furnished marshals, constables, and generals for the crown of France; like the Courtenays, they went *outre mer* for crowns. Gauthier de Brienne was King of Sicily and Duke of Apulia. John himself, one of the last specimens of the great crusading heroes, was titular King of Jerusalem, having married Constance, daughter of Isabelle and granddaughter of Amaury.[1] Philip Augustus himself selected John de Brienne as the most worthy knight to become the husband of Constance and the King of Jerusalem. He was now an old man of more than seventy years. His daughter, Yolande, was

[1] The following genealogy explains the succession of the crown of Jerusalem. It is taken from Baldwin II., who was a cousin of Godfrey and Baldwin I.

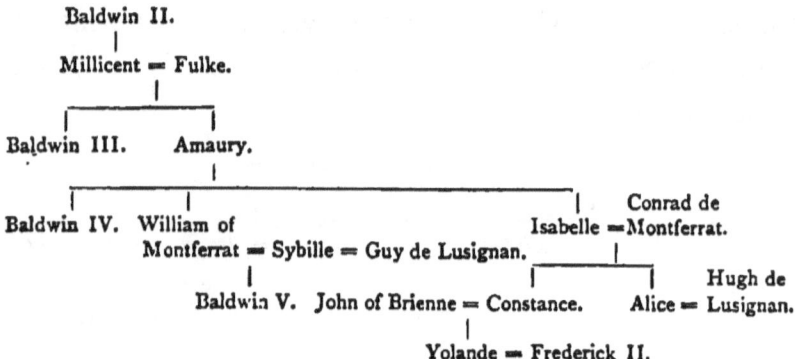

married to Frederick II., who had assumed the title of King of Jerusalem. But old as he was, he was still of commanding stature and martial bearing. His arm had lost none of its strength, nor his brain any of its vigour. He accepted the crown on the understanding that the young Baldwin, then eleven years of age, should join him as emperor on coming of age.

Great things were expected from so stout a soldier. Yet for two years nothing was done. Then the emperor was roused into action.

It was understood at Constantinople that Vatatces, the successor of Theodore Lascaris, was on the point of concluding an alliance, offensive and defensive, with Agan, King of the Bulgarians and successor of John. The alliance could have but one meaning, the destruction of the Latin empire. It must be remembered that the vast Roman empire of the East was shrunken in its dimensions to the city of Constantinople and that narrow strip of territory commanded by her walls, her scanty armies, and her diminished fleets. Of territory, indeed, the Latin empire had none in the sense of lands producing revenue. What they held, was held with the drawn sword in the hand ready for use. The kingdom of Thessalonica was gone; and though the Dukedoms, Marquisates, and Countships of Achaia, Athens, Sparta, and other independent petty states were still held by the emperors or their sons, they were like the outlying provinces of the Latin kingdom of Jerusalem, Edessa, Tripoli, and the rest, a source of weakness rather than of strength. Little help, if any, could be looked for from them.

Of course the Latin empire of Constantinople was a thing which never ought to have existed, and which could not, in the nature of things, endure. Like its predecessor of Jerusalem, it maintained an uncertain existence by continually attracting recruits from the West. When the supply of men began to fail; when the attention of France was diverted by the holy wars of their saintly King Louis; when Flanders was exhausted, or when the Flemish sympathies perished with the death of Henry, then the end of the empire was not far distant. The early deaths of the knights show, too, how fatal was the climate and the life.

The alliance, however, was concluded, and the allies, with an immense army, estimated at a hundred thousand, besides three hundred ships of war, sat down before the city and besieged it by sea and land. The incident that follows reads like a story from the history of Amadis de Gaul. Gibbon says that he "trembles" to relate it. While this immense host lay outside his walls; while thirty ships armed with their engines of war menaced his long line of seaward defences in the narrow strait, brave old John de Brienne, who had but 160 knight, with their following of men-at-arms and archers —say a couple of thousand in all—led forth his little band, and at one furious onset routed the besieging army. Probably it was mainly composed of the Bulgarian hordes, undisciplined, badly armed, and, like all such hosts, liable to panic. Perhaps, too, the number of the enemy was by no means so great as is reported, nor were the forces of John de Brienne so small. There is no necessity to detract from what was clearly as gallant a fight as was ever fought, but heroic proportions which are credible and possible are more likely to be accepted than those which belong only to a giant. Nor was his success limited to the rout of the army, for the citizens, encouraged by their flight, attacked the ships, and succeeded in dragging five and twenty of them within the port. It would appear that the Bulgarians renewed their attempt in the following year, and were again defeated by the old emperor. It would have been well for the Latins had his age been less. He died in the year 1237, and young Baldwin, who was married to his daughter Martha, became sole emperor. John de Brienne made so great a name, that he was compared with Ajax, Odin the Dane, Hector, Roland, and Judas Maccabæus. Baldwin, who came after him, might have been compared with any of those kinglings who succeeded Charlemagne, and sat in their palaces while the empire fell to pieces.

His incapacity is proved, if by nothing else, by his singular and uniform ill-luck. If after the fight of life is over, no single valiant blow can be remembered, the record is a sorry one indeed. Baldwin's difficulties were, it must be owned, very great: they were so great, that for a considerable portion of the four and twenty years during which he wore the Roman purple his crown was left him by sufferance. And his manner of reigning was to travel about Europe begging for money. The pope proclaimed a Crusade for him, but it was extremely difficult to awaken general enthusiasm for a Courtenay in danger of being overthrown by a Lascaris; and the other point, the submission of Constantinople to Rome in things ecclesiastical, could not be said to touch the popular sentiment at all. The Pope, however, supplemented his exhortation by bestowing upon the indigent emperor a treasure of indulgences, which he no doubt sold at their marketable value, whatever that was. One fears that it was not much. From England he obtained, after an open insult at Dover, the sum of 700 marks, which, at the purchasing value we have estimated roughly,[1] represents about £12,500, a small contribution towards the maintenance of an empire. Louis IX. of France would have rendered him substantial assistance, but for the more pressing claims of the Holy Land and his project for delivering the Holy Places by a new method. His brother-in-law, Frederick II., excommunicated by the Church, was not likely to manifest any enthusiasm for an ecclesiastical cause; and those allies from whom he might have expected substantial aid, the Venetians, were at war with the Genoese; the Prince of Achaia was in captivity, and the feeble son of Boniface, King of Thessalonica (the sons of all these sturdy Crusaders were feeble, like the Syrian *pullani*, sons of Godfrey's heroes) had been deposed. Yet money and men must be raised, or the city must be abandoned. A wise man would have handed over the empire to any who dared defend it. Baldwin was not a wise man. He proceeded to sell the remaining lands of Courtenay and the marquisate of Namur, and by this and other expedients managed to return with an army of 30,000 men.

[1] See page 164.

What would not Baldwin I., or Henry his uncle, or John de Brienne his father-in-law, have been able to effect with an army of 30,000 soldiers of the West? But Baldwin the Incapable did next to nothing.

By this time the strip of country remaining to the emperor was only that immediately surrounding the city. All the rest was in the hands of Greek or of Bulgarian. When these were at war, the city was safe; when these were united, the city was every moment in danger of falling.

Baldwin used his new recruits in gaining possession of the country for a distance of three days' journey round his capital—about sixty miles in all—which was something. But how was the position to be maintained, or to be improved? There were no revenues in that bankrupt city, from whose port the trade had passed away, and which had lost the command of the narrow seas. What was the condition of the citizens, we know not. That of the imperial household was such, that the emperor's servants were fain to demolish empty houses for fuel, and to strip churches of the lead upon their roofs to supply the daily wants of his family. He sent his son Philip to Venice as security for a debt; he borrowed at enormous interest of the merchants of Italy; and when all else failed, and the money which he had raised at such ruinous sacrifices had melted away, and his soldiers were clamouring for pay, he remembered the holy relics yet remaining to the city, in spite of the cartloads carried off during the great sack of 1204, and resolved to raise more money upon them.

There was, first of all, the Crown of Thorns. This had been already pledged in Venice for the sum of 13,134 pieces of gold to the Venetians. As the money was spent and the relic could not be redeemed within the time, the Venetians were preparing to seize it. They would have been within their right. But Baldwin conceived an idea, so clever that it must have been suggested by a Greek, which, if successfully carried out, would result in the attainment of much more money by its means. He would *give* it to Louis IX. of France. A relic of such importance might be pawned, it might be given, but it could not be sold. Therefore Baldwin gave it to King Louis. By this plan the Venetians were tricked of their relic, on which they had counted; the debt was transferred to France, which easily paid it; the precious object itself, to which Frederick II. granted a free passage through his dominions, was conveyed by Dominican friars to Troyes, whither the French court advanced to receive it, and a gift of 10,000 marks reconciled Baldwin and his barons to their loss. After all, as the prospects of the State were so gloomy, it might be some consolation to them to reflect that so sacred a relic—which had this great advantage over the wood of the True Cross, that it had not been and could not be multiplied until it became equal in bulk to the wood of a three-decker—was consigned to the safe custody of the most Christian King of France.

This kind of traffic once begun, and proving profitable, there was no reason why it should not continue. Accordingly, the Crown of Thorns was followed by a large and very authentic piece of the True Cross. St. Louis gave Baldwin 20,000 marks as an honorarium for the gift of this treasure, which he deposited in the Sainte Chapelle. Here it remained, occasionally working miracles, as every bit of the True Cross was bound to do, until the troubles of the League, when it was mysteriously stolen. Most likely some Huguenot laid hands upon it, and took the same kind of delight in burning it that he took in throwing the consecrated wafer to the pigs.

And then more relics were found and disposed of. There was the baby linen of our Lord; there was the lance which pierced His side; there was the sponge with which they gave Him to drink; there was the chain with which His hands had been fettered; all these things, priceless, inestimable, wonder-working, Baldwin sent to Paris in exchange for marks of silver. And then there were relics of less holiness, but still commanding the respect and adoration of Christians—these also were hunted up and sent. Among them were the rod of Moses, and a portion—alas! a portion only—of the skull of John the Baptist. Thirty or forty thousand marks for all these treasures. And it seems but a poor result of the conquest of Constantinople by the Latins that all which came of it was the transference of relics from the East to the West. Nothing else. Such order as the later Greek emperors had preserved, changed into anarchy and misrule; such commerce as naturally flowed from Asia into the Golden Horn, diverted and lost; a strange religion imposed upon an unwilling people; the break up of the old Roman forms; the destruction by fire of a third of the city; the disappearance of the ancient Byzantine families; the ruin of the wealthy; the depression of the middle classes; the impoverishment of the already poor; the decay and loss of learning; these were the things which the craft and subtlety of Dandolo, working on the Franks' lust of conquest, had brought about for the proud city of the East.

But the end was drawing daily nearer.

Vatatces of Nicæa died. He was succeeded by his son Theodore, on whose death the crown of Nicæa devolved upon an infant. The child was speedily, though not immediately, openly dethroned by the regent, Michael Palæologus. When at length the imperial title was assumed by the latter, Baldwin thought it advisable to attempt negotiations with him. His ambassadors were received with open contumely. Michael would give the Latins nothing. "Tell your master," he said, "that if he be desirous of peace, he must pay me, as an annual tribute, the sum which he receives from the trade and customs of Constantinople. On these terms I may allow him to reign. If he refuses, it will be war."

That was in the year 1259.

Michael, no putter forth of empty and boastful words, prepared immediately for the coming war. So in his feeble way did Baldwin. But his money was spent, his recruits were melting away, the Venetians alone were his allies, and the Genoese had joined the Greeks. And yet Michael did not know—so great was the terror of the Frank and Flemish name which the great Baldwin, Henry of Flanders, and John de Brienne had left behind them—how weak was the Latin empire, how unstable were the defences of the city.

Michael (A.D. 1260) marched into Thrace, strengthened the garrisons, and expelled the Latins yet remaining in the country. Had he, the same year, marched upon Constantinople, the city would have been his. But the glory of taking the city was destined for one of his generals.

The Greek emperor, returning to Nicæa, sent Alexis Strategopoulos, his most trusted general, on whom he had conferred the title of Cæsar, to take the command of his armies in Europe. He laid strict orders upon him to enter the Latin territory as soon as the existing truce was concluded; to watch, report, act upon the defensive, if necessary, but nothing more.

Now the lands round Constantinople had been sold by their Latin seigneurs to Greek cultivators, who, to defend their property, formed themselves into an armed militia, called voluntaries. With these voluntaries Alexis opened communications, and was by their aid enabled to get accurate information of all that went on among the Latins. As soon as the truce expired, he marched his troops across the frontier, and approached the city. His force—doubtless the Latins were badly served by their spies—seemed too small to inspire any serious alarm, and the Latins, who had recently received succour from Venice which made them confident, resolved on striking the first blow by an attack on the port of Daphnusia. They accordingly despatched a force of 6,000 men, with thirty galleys, leaving the city almost bare of defenders.

This, then, was the moment for successful treachery. One Koutrilzakes, a Greek voluntary, secured the assistance of certain friends within the town. Either a subterranean passage was to be opened to the Greeks, or they were to be assured of friends upon the walls. Alexis at dead of night brought his army close to the city. At midnight, against a certain stipulated spot the scaling-ladders were placed, where there were none but traitors to receive the men; at the same time, the passage was traversed, and Alexis found himself within the walls of the city. By a similar manœuvre did the Spaniards rob King René, two hundred years later, of his city of Naples. They broke open the Gate of the Fountain; they admitted the Greek men-at-arms and the Coman auxiliaries before the alarm was given; and by daylight the Greeks had complete command of the land wall, and were storming the imperial palace. There was one chance left for Baldwin. He might have betaken himself to the Venetians, and held their quarter until the unlucky expedition to Daphnusia returned, when they might have expelled the Greeks, or made at least an honourable capitulation. But Baldwin was not the man to fight a lost or losing battle. He hastily fled to the port, embarked on board a vessel, and set sail for Eubœa. In the deserted palace the Greek soldiers found sceptre, crown, and sword, the imperial insignia, and carried them in mockery through the streets.

While Baldwin was flying from the palace to the port,

behind him and around him was the tramp of the rude Coman barbarians, proclaiming that the city was taken. The houses, hastily thrown open as the first streaks of the summer day lit up the sky, resounded with the acclamations of those, yesterday his own subjects, who welcomed the new comers with cries of "Long live Michael the Emperor of the Romans!" The House of Courtenay had played its last card and lost the game. Pity that it was thrown away by so poor a player.

It matters little about the end of Baldwin. He got safely to Euboea, thence to Rome, and lived twelve or thirteen years longer in obscurity. When he died, his only son Philip assumed the empty title of emperor of Constantinople, which, Gibbon says, "too bulky and sonorous for a private name, modestly expired in silence and oblivion." It took, however, a long time to expire. Two hundred and fifty years later one of its last holders was the inheritor of so many shadowy claims that his very name in history is blurred by them. René of Anjou gave himself, among other titles, that of emperor of Constantinople.

Constantinople was taken, and the Latin empire destroyed at a blow. There were, however, still remaining the Venetian merchants, who had the command of the port, and who might, by holding out until the return of the ships from Daphnusia, undo all. Alexis set fire to their houses, but was careful to leave their communications with the vessels unmolested. They had therefore nothing left but to secure the safety of their wives, families, and movable property, which they did by embarking them on board the ships. And when the Daphnusian expedition returned, they found to their surprise that the Greeks held the whole city except a small portion near the port, and had manned the walls. A hasty truce was arranged; the merchants loaded every ship with their families and their property; the Latin fleet sailed down the Dardanelles, and the Latin empire in the East was at an end.

It began with violence and injustice: it ended as it began. There were six Latin Emperors, of whom the first was a gallant soldier; the second, a sovereign of admirable qualities, and an able administrator; the third, a plain French knight, who was murdered on his way to assume the purple buskins; the fourth, a weak and pusillanimous creature; the fifth, a stout old warrior; and the last a monarch of whom nothing good can be said and nothing evil, except that which was said of Boabdil, called El Chico, that he was unlucky; and bad luck is another name for incapacity. As the Latins never had the slightest right or title to these possessions in the East, so the Western powers were never impelled to assist them, and their downfall was merely a matter of time. In the interests of civilisation their occupation of the city seems to have been unfortunate; they learned nothing for themselves, they taught nothing; neither East nor West profited. They destroyed the old institutions, so that the ancient Roman Empire was broken up by their conquest; they inflicted irreparable losses on learning and art; and perhaps the only good result of their conquest was that for the moment at least it deflected the course of trade with the East from the Golden Horn, and sent it by another route to Venice, Genoa, and Pisa. As for the substitution of the Latin for the Greek Church, the change was only one from a blind and literal formalism to a blind and ignorant subjection to priestcraft.

CHAPTER XI.

THE LAST EMPERORS.

THE Byzantime empire would seem to have been endued with an almost miraculous vitality. Its capture and sack by the ruthless Latins might have been expected utterly and finally to extinguish it. Yet it was destined to survive the Latin conquest, and to see the downfall of the kingdom which for little better than half a century had usurped its place. Again it lifted its head, and for two more centuries Roman emperors, Cæsars as they were styled by their subjects and by the world, reigned with some outward splendour and some real power at Constantinople.

During these its last years, however, it painfully exhibited the infirmities of extreme old age. It was indeed "the sick man;" its ultimate recovery, it was unmistakably plain, was out of the question. The Turks under the House of Othman were conquering Asia Minor and menacing Europe early in the fourteenth century. Constantinople, it is true, had successfully resisted foes as barbarous and as formidable. But in those days she possessed resources of which she had now been stripped.

She was still wealthy, and the centre of a vast commerce; she could send numerous and well-equipped armies into the field, and her fleets, though once, as we have seen, worsted by Genseric and his Vandals, were powerful enough to command the Euxine and guard her possessions in the Mediterranean. Now all was changed. The Latin Crusader had spoiled and wasted her beyond the possibility of her ever again attaining the pre-eminent wealth and grandeur which had made her seem to be almost a worthy seat of the Cæsars. Her harbour was not crowded with merchant ships, as of old, and her suburbs were no longer the chosen residences of wealthy families from all parts of the world. The republics of Venice and Genoa had succeeded to her riches and her maritime power. The suburb of Galata or Pera was granted by the emperor who, in 1261, restored the Greek empire at Constantinople, as a possession to the Genoese, who had concluded an alliance with the Greeks, and had promised their naval assistance, at least for the defence of their capital. Established in this quarter, which they were to hold as the emperor's vassals on the usual terms of such a tenure, they soon by their enterprise drew into their own hands the commerce of the surrounding seas, and made themselves in fact independent of their nominal head.

The emperor to whom we have referred was the Michael Palæologus whom we have already had occasion to mention. We can but glance briefly at the events of his reign and at those of his successors. Of those events the chief, as far as the Byzantine empire is concerned, was the progress and conquests of the Turks. It was becoming evident that against this new power the empire would not be able to hold its own without vigorous support from the West. It was the anxious endeavour of some of the last emperors to procure a union between East and West, and one of them, Manuel, even visited France, Germany, and England, as a suppliant, pleading in the name of a common Christianity for resistance to the arms of the " infidel."

It was in the July of 1261, just as Baldwin and the Latins were on the point of flight, that we may say that Michael began his reign as a Byzantine emperor. He had indeed been crowned two years before at Nicæa, but now he was to enter the capital of his empire in triumph, and to hear from Greeks and Genoese the shout, " Long life and victory to Michael and John, the august emperors of the Romans!" John, the son of the late Emperor Theodore Lascaris, was at the time a boy of about eleven years of age. In the course of a few months he passed away into oblivion, his sight having been first destroyed by the singular device of confronting his eyes with the blinding glare of red-hot metal. For three years Michael lay under a sentence of excommunication from the patriarch of Constantinople, Arsenius, who, as the young prince's guardian, resented the crime, and, as a man with a strong sense of duty, thus publicly denounced it. In vain the emperor begged for absolution. He could only get Arsenius removed, and an obsequious monk elected in his room. Arsenius was respected both by people and clergy, and a prolonged schism was the result of his unjust treatment.

Michael found his capital an impoverished and well-nigh ruined city. The Latins during the last days of their occupation had not spared even the churches, and the Franks had polluted the palace with their drunken orgies. Michael applied himself vigorously to the work of restoration, and conciliated the traders of Genoa, Venice, and Pisa, by confirming the charters previously granted to them. He did everything he could to restore the commerce of Constantinople. He showed vigour, too, in recovering for the empire some of its lost territories. Lesbos, Chios, and Rhodes, and other islands of the Archipelago which had been comprised in the Byzantine dominions, were reconquered from the Latins; but the Asiatic provinces of the empire were neglected and left to the mercy of the advancing power of the Turks. There was again also danger from a possible Latin coalition. Charles of Anjou had allied himself with Philip, son of the Emperor Baldwin, with Pope Martin IV., and the Venetians, and an expedition was to be made from Brindisi for the attack of Constantinople. But all ended in failure. A rash and premature attempt at invasion was made by a small body of knights, who were utterly overwhelmed by a Greek army at Belgrade. The designs of Charles recoiled on himself. Sicily was lost to him in 1282, the year of the "Sicilian Vespers," and the Greek emperor, who died that same year, saw both safety assured to his capital and his enemy thoroughly humbled.

The two following reigns—those of Andronicus II., Michael's son, and of his grandson, Andronicus III., or the Younger—bring us down to the year 1341. The first reign covers a period of fifty years, for which we have indeed abundant historical materials; but the story, as Gibbon says, is a "languid as well as a prolix" one. The emperor was a very different man from his father, who certainly had vigour and ability, though when it served his purpose he could be both cruel and treacherous. Andronicus had a reputation for learning, and he was perhaps a really conscientious man. He was, however, unfortunately priestridden, and his religion was too much that of the mere monk and ecclesiastic. He was not at all a man of the world, and never ought to have been at the head of a small principality, much less of what still claimed to be an empire. After the fashion of his day he made his son Michael his colleague, but the young man, though styled emperor for twenty-five years, was of no service to the state either as a leader of its armies or as a director of its politics. All that could be said of him was that he was docile and well behaved. He had, however, a son, Andronicus the Younger, afterwards emperor, on whom even this negative praise could not be bestowed. Brought up in the palace with the idea that he was heir to the empire, he at first impressed his grandfather with the belief that he was a youth of singular promise, but he soon disgusted the strict and parsimonious old man by riotous living, and by contracting heavy debts with the Genoese money-lenders of Pera. Finally, when he found that he had hopelessly lost his grandfather's favour, and was to be excluded from the throne, he set up the standard of rebellion at Adrianople, and had as his abettor John Cantacuzenus, then the chief imperial minister, and subsequently his successor on the throne. He contrived, it is said, to muster a force of 50,000 troops, far larger, in fact, than could be brought into the field against the foreign enemies who were threatening the remnants of the empire. Civil war, or rather three consecutive civil wars, during a miserable seven years, was the immediate result. In 1328 the old emperor abdicated, asking only his life from his victorious grandson. For a while he lived in the palace, with the name of emperor and a liberal pension. His end was one which will not surprise us. From being a royal prisoner in the hands of keepers who despised and at last even threatened him, he became, or was forced into becoming, a monk, and under the changed name Antonius he died four years after his abdication.

His grandson's reign of thirteen years was a period of rapid decay for the empire. The younger Andronicus was already a worn-out man of pleasure, and he seems to have been quite indifferent to the public misfortunes. He was twice married, his first wife being the daughter of a duke of Brunswick, the head of a petty principality in the north of Germany, and his second the sister of the count of Savoy, who was crowned empress in the Greek Church of St. Sophia under the name of Anne. The time was when such alliances would have been spurned by a Byzantine emperor, but the Latin conquest and empire had somewhat lowered the pride of the "Roman Cæsar." Soon, as we shall see, he would have to stoop to the humiliation of craving succour from powers which his predecessors had disdained as barbarous.

It had been prophesied in his last moments by a senator during Michael's reign that the re-establishment of the Greek empire at Constantinople would prove the ruin of Asia. The irruptions of the Mogul Tartars into Europe and Asia Minor were a terrible but a comparatively brief calamity, and the senator's prophecy was not fulfilled till the Mogul had made way for the Turk. The reign of the elder Andronicus saw the advance of the Turks up to the shores of the Bosporus. The mountain passes of Bithynia, which ought to have been guarded by a local militia, had been neglected, and in the year 1299 Othman, the founder of the dynasty and empire named after him, approached the coasts of the Propontis near Nicomedia, of old the chief city of Bithynia. Prusa (Broussa), destined to be a well-known name in Eastern history, surrendered to his son Orchan in the same year, and its capture may be said to mark the first beginning of the Ottoman empire. A rapid advance was now made in these parts, and the reign of the younger Andronicus was particularly inglorious for the Greek empire. The emperor, however, fond of ease and pleasure as he was, did take the field, and encountered his new enemy, but only to be defeated and to lose the cities of Nicæa and Nicomedia, which for centuries had been under the Byzantine sway. Nearly all the western shores of the Archipelago had been already wrested from the empire. The Roman province of Asia, in fact, was now once for all lost to it, and its old cities, with their relics of past greatness and of Greek civilization, were reduced to poverty-stricken villages. The invader had no sympathy with what we admire and regret. He desolated and destroyed as well as conquered, as the condition of the country in our day mournfully attests. The noble and once flourishing city of Ephesus now perished, and it is but in our own generation that some ruins of its famous temple have at last been brought to light by the patient industry of Mr. Wood. Heathen and Christian antiquity alike were almost effaced, and the wasting of this beautiful and historic region is one of the most painful chapters in the history of the world.

While all this miserable work was being done, the empire was torn, as we have seen, by civil strife between the elder and younger Andronicus. But for the feeble effort of the latter at resistance, the enemy went quite unchecked, and the Turkish chiefs (emirs as they were called) were now beginning to harass with their ships the islands of the Mediterranean and the Greek shores. But it was not till some years afterwards that we can say that the Turks established themselves in Europe. A strange incident had meanwhile occurred. The daughter of John Cantacuzenus, the minister who had supported the younger Andronicus against his grandfather, had been given in marriage to Orchan, now become for a time the emperor's ally. The friendship and alliance of the Turk involved the condition that he might sell his prisoners of war as slaves at Constantinople, and we hear of Christians, both men and women, being sold by public auction. Yet the interval between this infamy and the end of all was longer than we might have expected. It seems that Orchan, with barbaric cunning, completely outwitted the imperial ministers, and became master of some fortresses in Thrace, and of the commanding position of Gallipoli. Cantacuzenus saw that a stronger power was rapidly pushing aside the decrepit empire, and in his last counsels advised his Greek subjects to bow to inevitable fate. His advice may have been prudent, but it is some satisfaction to find that it was not followed. The Greeks or some of them still clung to the hope of saving the poor remains of their empire. But Orchan's son and successor, Amurath I., by whom the famous force of the janissaries was at least regularly organised, if not actually created, won a series of easy triumphs, and his arms in Europe and in Asia left Constantinople utterly isolated, and, as we may suppose, quite at his mercy. John Palæologus was emperor only in name. He was Amurath's vassal, and he and his sons had to dance attendance, in court and camp, on the mighty barbarian. If he was to be saved from this degradation, he must appeal to the pope or the Western powers, and even from this quarter deliverance would be by no means certain.

His predecessor, Cantacuzenus, who, like the elder Andronicus, had ended his days in the retirement of the cloister, attempted through Pope Clement VI. to arrange a reconciliation between the East and the West, with a view to the strengthening of the Greek empire. He had, as we have said, almost betrayed its interests by his friendship with Orchan, to whom he had married his daughter, and now his endeavours to undo the mischief of having let the Turkish power establish itself in Europe were all in vain. John Palæologus, whose long reign of thirty-six years, from 1355 to 1391, witnessed the unmistakable signs of impending downfall, made similar attempts with no better success. He is to be remembered as the first of the emperors who himself went a suppliant to the pope at Rome, begging help against the infidel. After having duly kissed the pontiff's hands and feet, and led his mule by the bridle, he was feasted in the Vatican, but he had to leave it with very little encouragement. Pope Urban V. could not revive the enthusiasm of the age of the Crusades, and the emperor was obliged to return in bitter disappointment. He had to pass through Venice, and here he found himself in a miserably ridiculous plight. On his way to Rome he had borrowed largely from the Venetian bankers and money-lenders, and now, as he was unable to pay, his creditors held his person in pawn. His brother Manuel was generous enough to become his security, and by selling and mortgaging all he possessed, he satisfied their claims, and enabled the emperor to return to his capital, whence during the remainder of his reign he had to look on quietly while his empire was being narrowed down by the conquests of Amurath to the mere precincts of the city.

His son Manuel succeeded him, and reigned from 1391 to 1425. Manuel from boyhood must have been well drilled in lessons of humiliation, as with his father and his brother he had been an attendant in court and camp on the barbarian monarch. At the time of his father's death he was a hostage in the hands of Bajazet, Amurath's son and successor, and was living in his palace at Broussa. Thence he contrived to escape, and hurried to Constantinople. The Turk, a savage warrior of the most furious energy,[1] gave him a brief respite, and completed meanwhile his father's conquests in Europe and Asia. Then at last he sent Manuel a letter, bidding him resign his capital, or tremble for himself and his people. However, he graciously allowed the poor emperor to purchase a truce of ten years, one of the inglorious conditions of which was that there was to be a mosque in Constantinople. But even this truce was too much for the impatient Bajazet, and now Manuel's sole resource was to seek help from the West. The duke of Burgundy and the young princes of France, with Sigismund, king of Hungary, and a host of German knights, fought with impetuous ardour for Christendom in this extremity, and would have won the day but for their overweening confidence and the overwhelming numbers of the barbarian cavalry. The battle of Nicopolis, in 1396, was fiercely contested, and the janissaries had to yield to the chivalry of the West. But in the end Bajazet's victory was decisive, and the duke of Burgundy and the French princes became his prisoners. The peril to Constantinople was now again imminent, and but for the rapid movements of Tamerlane, who was now threatening the newly-acquired Ottoman possessions, it must have fallen. In 1400 Manuel quitted the city, and for two years was a voluntary exile. He was a suppliant at the courts of France, England, and Germany, but with no result. He was courteously and hospitably entertained, and received the honour due to an emperor.

[1] He was surnamed the Lightning.

Henry IV. of England was particularly attentive to him, and almost encouraged him to believe that he would give him something more than mere sympathy. But the circumstances of Western Europe were altogether unfavourable to his views. It was the time of the great schism, when the Church was divided between rival popes at Rome and Avignon. Manuel, however, on his return, found himself delivered from his worst fears. The terrible Tartar conqueror, after carrying his destructive arms from Russia to India, had struck down the sultan—a title which Bajazet was the first of the House of Othman to assume—in a great battle in the plains round the city of Angora. Bajazet was utterly overthrown, and according to the old story which has made his name memorable, lived for years in captivity, a prisoner in an iron cage.[1] Tamerlane's victory was a piece of great good fortune for Manuel. The Ottoman conquests were stayed at least for a time, and Bajazet's five sons seemed bent on undoing the work of their father by strife among themselves. Asiatic dynasties, as Gibbon has truly observed, present "an unceasing round of valour, greatness, discord, degeneracy, and decay." In this instance the Ottoman power speedily recovered itself under a prince of unquestionable capacity and some really great qualities, who perhaps deserved success, Amurath II (Murad). But its temporary eclipse after the fall of Bajazet gave the empire a little breathing space, and even a transient gleam of prosperity. Some of the Ottoman conquests were lost, and a few of the cities of Thessaly and Mace-

[1] The cage was probably nothing but a covered litter.

donia were surrendered to the emperor. One of Bajazet's sons, Mousa, who with his father had been taken prisoner at the battle of Angora, did indeed threaten Constantinople both by land and sea. But his fleet was defeated, and his attempt on the city by land resolved itself into nothing more than a few skirmishes under the walls, and could not be called a siege. Manuel, however, was by no means hopeful as to the future, and in speaking about his son to his chief minister, Phranza, the last of the Byzantine historians, he intimated that the time for an emperor was past, and that "a cautious steward was needed for the relics of empire." Acting on this principle, he tried to secure some advantages by a cunning diplomacy, and to recover Gallipoli by supporting the designs of Mustapha, a pretended son of Bajazet, then at Constantinople. His idea was to undermine the strength of the Ottoman by encouraging dynastic quarrels. But his arts failed him. Mustapha, having got Gallipoli, would not cede it to the emperor, saying that he could not give up what was now a Mussulman town. After some successes he was deserted by his partisans, and was taken prisoner and hanged by Amurath. Manuel's unfortunate intrigue soon brought trouble on him. Amurath laid siege to Constantinople with an army, it is said, of 200,000 men, and with some rude specimens of artillery, now used by the Turks for the first time. The city's defences had been strengthened, it appears, by the late Emperor John, and it was now well able to defy the sultan's clumsy cannon, and an assault headed by a famous dervish was repulsed with very trifling loss to the defenders. Of the janissaries, the flower of the assailing army, upwards of a thousand were slain; while of the besiegers, who fought almost in safety from their walls, both killed and wounded did not exceed a hundred and thirty. The siege had been begun in the June of 1422, and lasted two months, and then the sultan, who under different circumstances would no doubt have prolonged it, was hurried back to Broussa by tidings of his brother's revolt. He did not again attack Constantinople. The emperor and sultan concluded a peace, the terms of which were fairly favourable to the former, who, though he had to pay a considerable tribute, still numbered among his possessions Thessalonica and some towns in Thrace. He lived to a good old age, and died in the year 1425, having, after the manner of the Palæologi, become a monk towards his life's close.

His son, John Palæologus II., had, it is said, during his father's lifetime shown signs of a rather enterprising disposition. These Manuel, as we have seen, decidedly discouraged, as ill-suited to the age and even pregnant with danger to the empire, which in his opinion could hope only for a very tame and quiet existence. John, from 1425 to 1448, reigned quite on sufferance as the vassal and tributary of the sultan. Whatever may have once been his thoughts and aspirations, he now contentedly acquiesced in the humble position of "a cautious steward of empire." At the Council of Florence, 1438, he and the patriarch of Constantinople, with the Greek bishops, submitted themselves to the Latin Church; but the ecclesiastics on their return had to repudiate this submission, and were themselves despised and distrusted alike by their own people and the Latins, whom they had wished to conciliate. If the emperor had ever allowed himself to hope for support from the West against the Turk, he must soon have been convinced of his self-deception. It might have once for a brief space seemed possible that the Ottoman power would fall before Ladislaus, king of Hungary, and his brave general, Huniades, but the battle of Varna in 1444 was a decisive victory for Amurath. The emperor thought it well to be civil to the victor, and sent to congratulate him on his success, and to beg that he might again be his friend and ally. His prayer was heard, and for four more years he lived to enjoy the sultan's favour.

We are now within five years of the end. With the reign of one more emperor Byzantine history finally closes. The last of the Cæsars was Constantine Palæologus, a name not inglorious, though associated with a fearful downfall. He was worthy of a happier age, and he perished, we shall see, like a hero, mindful of the empire he represented, and resolved to shed at least some glory on its dissolution. The brother of the late emperor, he succeeded to the throne at the mature age of fifty-four. At the time of his brother's death he was governing with the title of "despot" a little fragment of the empire in the Peloponnese, the defence of which he had maintained with some spirit and bravery against the Turks. He had two brothers still living, Demetrius and Thomas, and of these the former, as the elder and as "born in the purple," had a priority of claim, and he was supported by a party. But he was passed over, and the choice of nobles, clergy, and people fell on Constantine, who really deserved it. Their choice, however, was not enough to decide the matter. The sultan, whose tributary vassal the late emperor had been, must be consulted. Constantine himself, it appears, was not particularly eager to accept what he must have felt was little more than a barren honour. He may well have foreseen that very possibly he might be the last of the long line of so-called Roman emperors. It might be a question whether Amurath would even give him the chance, as he had dared to resist his arms during his government in the Peloponnese. The sultan held his court at Adrianople, and thither Phranza went as an ambassador to learn his wishes. With Amurath's assent Constantine was proclaimed emperor. He was crowned at Sparta in 1449.

Phranza, who was a few years younger than the emperor, had his full confidence and managed all business for him, "I am surrounded," said Constantine of his court, "by men whom I can neither love nor trust nor esteem." The Greek nobles of the last period of the empire seem, indeed, to have been a worthless set. They could, no doubt, now and then fight bravely when the capital itself was attacked. But in general they were quarrelsome and intriguing, cunning and mistrustful, and anything like patriotic feeling had quite died out from among them. The emperor, we may be pretty sure, was not too hard on them. Phranza was indeed a noble exception. He was not only an able man, as a minister and a diplomatist, but he appears to have been a really faithful servant. He must have known both Greeks and Turks thoroughly. He had been on many an embassy to the sultan, and more than once had outwitted his ministers. On one occasion he made them look very foolish by making them drunk at one of his entertainments, and then getting hold of some state papers in their possession. Having ascertained the contents, he quietly and politely put the papers back into the Turks' pockets. This is just what we might have expected from a Greek. Phranza, as a minister in a difficult time, must have been invaluable. He certainly is invaluable as a historian of a period which, but for his chronicle written long afterwards in a monastery in Corfu, would be much less distinctly known to us. It is indeed a great thing to have a contemporary record from a man who had so many excellent opportunities. Phranza witnessed with his own eyes the fall of Constantinople, and if his narrative is apt to be rather too prolix and grandiloquent, we may at any rate congratulate ourselves that the story of that memorable event as told by such an eyewitness has come down to us.

CHAPTER XII.

FALL OF CONSTANTINOPLE, A.D. 1453.

WHETHER Constantine was to be really the last of the Roman emperors, or whether the poor shrunken remains of what had been the grandest of empires were still fated to prolong their feeble and precarious existence, hung, it would seem, on two contingencies. If the Turk could not be permanently withstood, he might perhaps be stayed for a time, in the event of the sword of Othman passing into the hands of a weak or unambitious sovereign. To a barbarian power in its early advance, the character and capacity of a ruler are all important. The great and valiant Amurath, who had shaken with his artillery the walls of the city of the Cæsars, and had struck down on the field of Varna a Christian host led by the heroic John Huniades, died in 1451, and, as has often happened, might leave his sceptre to a weak and contemptible successor. There was another possibility. The Christian league which Pope Eugenius had formed, and which Amurath had baffled, might be revived, and who could say that this time it might not be successful? There would seem to be strong motives for such an effort. The Turk, with his savagery and unbelief, was, alike to Greeks and to Latins, the immediate precursor of that awful Antichrist of whose advent in the latter days prophets and apostles had so plainly warned the Church of Christ. And Constantinople, though its grandeur and glory had faded, and though its faith in Western opinion was tainted with heresy, might still, especially at such a crisis as the present, claim to be regarded as Sion—the city of God— as well as the heir of Roman traditions and civilisation. Rome could never quite disown her as a daughter, though she might have been disobedient and refractory; still less could she see her trampled under foot by the infidel without a sense of humiliation and self-reproach.

Nor could there be much doubt that Europe possessed resources amply sufficient to save the city, and even to push back the Turk into his proper home in Asia. When we look back upon the situation, we may well accept Gibbon's opinion, that "a moderate armament of the maritime states might have saved the relics of the Roman name, and maintained a Christian fortress in the heart of the Ottoman Empire." But one soon sees that there were many substantial reasons why the effort was not made. Europe was very different from what it had been three centuries ago. The thoughts and ideas of men had greatly changed. The religious enthusiasm which had responded to the preaching of Peter the Hermit had yielded before a new class of impulses. Social and political movements were coming to the front and stirring the popular mind. It would have been difficult for an eminently zealous and spirited pope to unite the Western States in anything like a Crusade against a power which as yet was not a direct menace to any one of them. There was a greater disposition to count the cost of an enterprise than there had been in the simpler and more credulous days of old. Nor was the papal throne filled by a man of any conspicuous vigour and enthusiasm. The Roman pontiff of the period, Nicholas V., in many respects worthily represented his high office; but he had neither ability nor inclination to make that supreme effort which alone could ward off the huge calamity impending over Christendom. He was not a man of action; he was a scholar, and a patron of scholars; and he spent the eight years of his pontificate in quietly collecting manuscripts of the classics, and in forming a library. He seems indeed to have felt that it was his duty to do something for the Greeks in their distress, and "he had it in his mind"—so it is courteously expressed by a writer of the time—"to help them." But his heart was clearly not in the matter. He did not in fact like the Greeks. Their duplicity towards the Latin Church, and their unwillingness to cast off their heresy and to unite themselves with Western Christendom on the prescribed conditions, had disgusted him. He had even gone so far as to prophesy their downfall and the conquest of their capital. We have to thank him that, as soon as he saw his prophecy accomplished, he did his best to rescue the relics of the Byzantine libraries; but it occurs to us to ask, with something of reproach, whether he might not have been the means of preserving for us the contents of those libraries, so far as they had survived the rough treatment of the city at the hands of the Latin Crusaders? Nor can we avoid the reflection that, had he acted—as was surely his duty—with more decision and promptitude, we might possibly have been spared that entail of perplexity and misery which we describe, and perhaps shall long have to describe, as "the Eastern question."

It may, however, be fairly admitted that Nicholas V. could not have seen much to encourage him in the general sentiments and attitude of Europe. He could hardly have appealed with much effect to England or to France. England, even if its people could have been brought to see and understand the nature of the crisis, which, in the absence of a powerful wave of religious enthusiasm, would have been hardly possible, was in the agony of a civil strife that absorbed all its energies. The rival Houses of York and Lancaster were infinitely more to the English people than the peril of a remote city on the Bosporus, which to nine-tenths of them must have been a mere name, could possibly be. France, indeed, might have been reasonably expected to feel that she had some interest, if not a very direct one, in saving Christendom from infidels and barbarians; and the French generally would have been fairly well acquainted with the name of Constantinople, and able in some degree to appreciate what the city represented, and the duty and importance of its preservation. Such an enterprise, if urged and encouraged by the pope, might have seemed to them honourable and glorious, and we can imagine that they might have been persuaded to embark on it. It is true that they were no longer animated by the old spirit of the Crusades, but French chivalry was still formidable and famous, and French volunteers, at the bidding of Pope Eugenius, had fought side by side with Poles and Hungarians in the battle of Varna. France, however, was thoroughly occupied with its own affairs. It had been brought very low by its recent struggle with England, and by its great defeat at Agincourt. Now it was recovering itself. England's domestic calamities during the Wars of the Roses were France's opportunity. Normandy from this time became once for all French territory, and King Charles VII. had the satisfaction of seeing his kingdom strengthened and consolidated. With this he was content, and having plenty of occupation at home, he was not likely to be moved to undertake a costly foreign expedition, which must have been a grievous hindrance to the progress his country was now making. Had the pope called on France for an effort, we may be sure that only a few French knights and gentlemen would have answered his appeal. Might he not have looked to Germany? There indeed was a country which could have sent forth a numerous and well-equipped host, powerful enough, we should suppose, to have thrust the Turk out of Europe; but it was a country divided into a number of kingdoms and principalities, and its people, though brave and warlike, were slow to move. The thing might perhaps have been accomplished if a man of spirit and energy had been its head. In the thirteenth century, when European civilisation was threatened by the Tartar hordes, and the barbarian inroads had reached Austria, the emperor, Frederic II., had very plainly pointed out to the kings of Europe and to the German princes the expediency of uniting their arms against the common enemy. Before the chivalry of France and Germany the savage multitude fell back into the remote wilds of Russia, and Western Europe was saved. It could hardly be said that the present peril was less pressing. Should the Turk wrest Constantinople from the Greeks, he would at once be entrenched in a position from which he would be able at any time to disquiet and alarm Christendom, and from which it would be next to impossible to dislodge him. But from Germany little was to be expected. It had a head no way fitted for the occasion. The emperor, Frederic III., was himself as tame and peace-loving as the Roman pontiff. Indeed, his chief claim to distinction is that he was the last of the German emperors who, by being crowned at Rome, acknowledged the pope's right to confirm the imperial title.

Bordering on Germany were the kingdoms of Poland and Hungary. These had a clear interest in making a stand against Turkish encroachment, and they proved an effectual barrier. But for their resolute resistance, the Turk might have considerably enlarged his dominions in Europe, and have established himself for at least a long period in Southern Germany. No people could be braver and more warlike than the Poles and Hungarians, who in this respect justified their affinity to the ancient Scythians; but their country was very poor, and a well-armed standing army was an impossibility for them. Domestic feuds, too, continually divided and distracted them, and only a king or chief of exceptional vigour could handle such material with much effect. They were able and willing to defend themselves against an invader, but it could hardly have been reasonable to expect that they would follow up and crush the invader on his own ground, and rescue distant cities and countries from his grasp. For this they had not sufficient discipline and organisation. Their best arm was their light cavalry, conspicuous for its reckless dash; but with this alone and unsupported they would have been no match for the strength and cohesion of such an army as Amurath could bring into the field. They had, however, at this time a brave young soldier-king in Ladislaus, and under him Poles and Hungarians were united. They had, too, a far greater man in the famous hero, John Huniades, the terror of the Turks, who has earned the everlasting gratitude of all Christian nations by his rescue of Belgrade from the clutches of the terrible conqueror of Constantinople. Christendom, shocked and dismayed by the fall of the capital of the East, and by the subsequent triumphs of the infidel, could after that achievement breathe more freely. But the resources of these Poles and Hungarians did not allow them to raise anything more than what the Romans called a "tumultuary" army, and such a force alone would clearly not have been equal to the occasion. There still remained the rich and powerful republics of Venice and Genoa. These maritime powers could do much, if they chose, and prompt and efficient aid might surely be expected from them. And they had strong motives for doing their utmost to save the last remnant of the Greek Empire. As great commercial communities, they had a direct interest in preserving for the Greeks the city which, as the principal dépôt of Eastern trade, was one of the main sources of their own wealth. It must, one would suppose, have been well worth their while to have strained their resources to the uttermost for the defence of Constantinople. Something indeed they did, but it was small compared with what by vigorous united action, and in the absence of jealousies and misunderstandings, might certainly have been accomplished. The decisive success which a small Genoese squadron achieved against the entire Turkish fleet during the siege, seems to imply that the will was wanting rather than the ability. Venice and Genoa might well, we are tempted to believe, have saved the city. That with the aid of the Western powers they could have done it, hardly admits of a question. But the aid was not forthcoming, and we have seen some of the reasons why it could not easily have been rendered. At the same time it was absolutely certain that Constantinople must fall without such aid, if the young sultan who succeeded Amurath was both able and aggressive.

Left to its own resources, the city was comparatively weak. Its defences had the reputation of being all but impregnable, and as a matter of fact they proved extremely formidable to the assailant. Phranza describes the landward defence as consisting of two walls, twenty-five feet in breadth, separated by an interval of thirty-two feet, and strengthened at numerous points by towers covered with a facing of lead. Approach to the outer wall was cut off by a wide and deep fosse. The inner wall was not in a thoroughly sound condition. It had been neglected, and what was worse, money intended for its repair had been misappropriated by the officials who had charge of the business. It might, it would seem, have been made an almost insuperable barrier against any enemy in the world. As it was, the walls were barely equal to sustaining the weight of the heavier pieces of ordnance which ought to have been mounted on them. Here was plain evidence of a neglect and apathy at such a time to the last degree base and criminal.

Had, however, the fortifications been perfect, there were not men in the city to garrison them. At the period of the Latin conquest the population was perhaps half a million ; now it had dwindled down to a hundred thousand, and of those certainly not more than seven or eight thousand could have passed as able-bodied soldiers. The two last centuries had been centuries of a miserable decline in all respects, and the latter half of the fourteenth century in particular had been a time of very rapid decay. Of this the Greeks themselves were distinctly conscious, and, as is the way with declining nations, they adopted foreign fashions, and borrowed the manners of Italians, ·Genoese, Venetians, and even of Turks. What remnant of empire they still possessed was for the most part occupied by a thin and poverty-stricken population, and everything outside the city walls wore a dreary and desolate aspect. Amurath completed their ruin, and after his siege a few open villages, tenanted by small farmers, were all that was left to the Greeks. And within the city itself were clearly visible the signs of feebleness and poverty, and of an utter absence of public spirit. The once magnificent streets, which amazed visitors from the West by their gorgeous display of wealth and luxury, now presented long ranges of ruined houses and palaces, from which the architectural glories of old, the marble columns and exquisite mosaics, had been purchased and carried away by the merchant princes of Venice and Genoa. Constantinople was, in fact, a ruined city. It is true, indeed that even in this period of swift and plainly-marked decay a Greek could, in a letter to the emperor, John Palæologus, boast in pompous phrases of its surviving splendour; but, as Gibbon observes, "a sigh and confession escape from the orator that his wretched country was but the shadow and sepulchre of its former self." The people, it would appear, had become too spiritless even to take common precautions against the frequent recurrence of famine and of pestilence. Between 1348 and 1418 the last-mentioned calamity is said to have afflicted the city eight times; and the first, as we might almost infer, came at frequent intervals. A specially deadly disease wrought terrible havoc among the citizens in the year 1431, some years after the siege by Amurath. After this we can hardly wonder that they had neither heart nor spirit, as indeed they had not adequate strength, for a resolute defence, should they be again menaced by such a foe.

We have a description of the state of Constantinople and its neighbourhood from a traveller who went thither in the following year. This was a knight from Burgundy, one Bertrandon de la Brocquière, who, as he was returning from a pilgrimage to Jerusalem, visited the famous city. Its fortifications struck him as formidable and imposing, but the interior distinctly revealed the most deplorable poverty and desolation; while without, the country was waste, and almost bare of inhabitants. Of the Greeks who yet remained, he gives anything but a flattering picture. "All with whom I have had any concern," he says, "have only made me more suspicious, for I have found more probity in the Turks." The race, there cannot be a doubt, had become wretchedly demoralised. From want of energy and industry they had let their trade slip from them into the hands of the Genoese, Venetians, and Italians, and frittered away their time in those petty trifling amusements which have a charm only for the weak and frivolous. Their ancestors delighted in the games of the hippodrome: these degenerate people found abundant pleasure in staring at royal processions and elaborate religious ceremonies. In their way, indeed, they were religious, and they prided themselves intensely on their orthodoxy. They were as exclusive as were the Pharisees. Latins and all Western Europeans they contemned as heretics; and one of their highest nobles, the Grand Duke Notanas, a typical Greek, declared that the turban of the sultan would be a more welcome sight to him in Constantinople than the tiara of the pope. They were infinitely too conceited to think that they might with advantage learn a few new lessons. They certainly might with considerable profit to themselves have taken a hint from their enemies, the Turks, whom their great Sultan Amurath had at least taught truth and honesty, as well as valour, by his own noble example. The Turk of those days was undoubtedly a favourable contrast to the Greek, and this was the conviction even of many Christians. The princes of the House of Othman really owed their successes, in part at least, to the superiority of their moral qualities. A Greek official was pretty sure to be greedy and corrupt. If he was proud of his city, he would hardly serve it or fight for it in an honest way. The state was miserably poor, but there were vast hoarded treasures in the possession of a few rich and selfish people, who paraded their fine furniture and wardrobes, and buried their superfluous wealth deep in the earth. In the very last struggle, the emperor could not find the means to pay his troops. He had to ransack the churches for plate and jewels, though his Greeks pretended to believe that their cathedral, St. Sophia, had been desecrated by the celebration within its sacred walls of the union of the Eastern and Western Churches. The people who grudged their blood and treasure in defence of the city of which they boasted as pre-eminently holy and divine, wrangled angrily with the Latins concerning the bread of the Lord's Supper, whether it should be leavened or unleavened, at the very moment when the common enemy of Christendom was thundering at their gates. "They would not have listened," says the historian Ducas, "to an angel from heaven, bidding them be at peace with Rome." It would seem that the popular and monastic sentiment was fanatical to a degree which even those who are most familiar with the extremes of religious bitterness would find it hard to realise. Some, indeed, of the higher ecclesiastics, who were no doubt men of culture, were free from this shocking infatuation, but the general tone of the citizens rendered patriotism impossible, and almost compels us to believe that they thoroughly deserved their fate.

The "great destroyer," as Gibbon calls Mahomet II., succeeded to his father Amurath at the age of twenty-one. To the emperor, who knew something of his tastes and character as a boy, he did not at first seem likely to be very formidable or dangerous. Constantine underrated his capacity, and perhaps now and then flattered himself with the idea of a brief respite for his city. He was soon undeceived. The young sultan began his reign with the murder of an infant brother, and with the maturer wisdom of his later years he obtained from his legal advisers a formal sanction of the practice of imperial fratricide for "his illustrious descendants, in order to secure the repose of the world." Then, it is said, he went on to murder certain ministers who had dissuaded his father from trusting him with power during his own lifetime. He could be, it was clear, savagely cruel, and it might be fairly presumed that he would be unscrupulous and perfidious; and now it began to be whispered that bad times were in store for the feeble and unfortunate

Greeks. He had, too, a cool head, and it was said of him that he was "as wise as his elders both in home affairs and in war." In his fashion he was fond of learning, and he at least liked the society of learned men, and could talk pleasantly with them, and if necessary discuss theology with a Christian patriarch. We might have expected that such a man's attainments would be prodigiously exaggerated. The story is told, but is hardly to be believed, that he was well acquainted with the Greek, Latin, Arabic, Persian, and Chaldee languages. He is also said to have been a very diligent reader, and to have delighted in the lives of Alexander, Augustus, Constantine, and Theodoric. Astrology, an important science at that time, and not necessarily repugnant to powerful intellects, was a study to which he was partial, and in which he had made great progress. He used to say that he knew by the planetary movements that he was destined to be a great conqueror. We may well believe that with his shrewd sagacity was mingled an alloy of superstition. Certain it is that in his early youth he developed that extravagant ambition which is often found to be combined with a firm belief in fate and destiny. Equally certain is it that the fury of his passions knew no restraint, and so foul was his licentiousness, that it is hard to admire his undoubted ability and farsightedness. To Phranza, after the fall of the city, he seemed almost a devil. To the historian Ducas he stood in marked contrast to his father Amurath, who "never wilfully destroyed any city or state, but was really averse to war, and a lover of peace." The son from childhood, he goes on to say, was "a dissembler, a wolf in sheep's clothing, an Antichrist before the final Antichrist, transformed, like Satan, into an angel of light." It was Mahomet's perfidy and cunning, more than his other vices, which seem to have scandalised the Greeks of his time. The Latin archbishop of Mitylene, Leonard of Chios, writing the story of the fall of the city three months afterwards in a letter addressed to the pope, saw in him the unmistakable instrument of Divine vengeance on those perverse Greeks who would not let themselves be cordially united to Rome. If the Greeks deserved their doom ever so much, we at any rate must number their conqueror among "the destroyers rightly called, and plagues of men."

There would seem to be no good reason for classing Mahomet with the few men of first-rate military genius who have appeared in the world. His great achievement, the conquest of Constantinople, was comparatively easy with the vast resources at his command. The way, as we have seen, had been thoroughly well prepared for him, and he had only to put a finishing stroke to a work which had long been in progress. While we may fairly credit him with immense energy and boundless ambition, we cannot justly compare him with an Alexander, a Cæsar, or a Hannibal. "He was," says Gibbon, "doubtless a soldier and possibly a general," and beyond this he does not seem worthy to be extolled. His conquests no doubt were on a considerable scale, and are said with Oriental exaggeration to have embraced ten kingdoms and two hundred cities. He certainly annexed to the Ottoman dominions the islands of Chios, Lesbos, Xante, and Cephalonia, and a part of Servia, while in his attacks on Cyprus and Rhodes he was unsuccessful. It must be remembered that he always had the advantage of vastly superior numbers, and yet he received more than one decisive check. He was driven in utter rout from the walls of Belgrade by Huniades. But as the conqueror of the city of the Cæsars he has won an everlasting fame, though one with which his actual exploits hardly seem commensurate.

The young sultan's position on his accession to power was not a very easy one. At the time of his father's death he was governing the province of Magnesia, but he was then instantly recalled to his European dominions by a message which showed plainly that a vigorous hand was at once needed in the new ruler. The janissaries had already assumed a threatening attitude. Mahomet lost no time in crossing the Hellespont and in hurrying to Adrianople. His promptitude had the desired effect; the janissaries were overawed and submissive, and both army and people welcomed as their sovereign the son of the great Amurath. Ambassadors came from the Western courts with courteous congratulations. The treaty with the emperor was solemnly renewed and ratified. The new sultan gave the impression that he intended to be a man of peace, and a scrupulous observer of all treaty obligations. Constantine must have breathed again, and had hopes that he might after all be spared the humiliation of witnessing the end.

Living at this time at the imperial court was a descendant of Sultan Bajazet's eldest son, who received a liberal pension for his maintenance from the Turks. The emperor requested, or rather demanded, that this allowance should be increased; and intimated that in the event of refusal he would let him leave Constantinople, and encourage him to set up a rival claim to the Turkish throne. It was almost an act of direct hostility, and one to which the new sultan, if a man of any spirit, could hardly be expected to submit. The old grand vizier of the late sultan, Khalil, who was still alive, and had a friendly feeling towards the Greeks, saw the danger. He well knew the temper of the young Mahomet, and he solemnly warned the emperor. "The scrupulous Amurath," he said to the imperial envoys, "is no more; his throne is occupied by a young conqueror whom no laws can bind and no obstacles can resist." Khalil seems to have been a just and peace-loving man, and as he gave good counsel to the emperor, so too he exerted his influence in endeavouring to dissuade the sultan from his designs against the Greek empire. Mahomet, himself, meanwhile showed no signs of wrath, but was as bland and conciliatory as ever. The emperor's envoys were dismissed with peaceful assurances and promises that Greek interests should be respected. But the sultan had seen his opportunity, and his plans were already formed. He had resolved from the first to complete his father's work, and to possess himself of Constantinople.

His first step was to put an end to the pension

received by the Ottoman prince at the imperial court. Next, he virtually began the siege of the city. A fortress had been erected by his grandfather Bajazet on the Asiatic side of the Bosporus, where its waters are narrowest, and his father Amurath is said to have vowed, after his victory at Varna, the erection of a similar fortress to confront it on the European shore. Mahomet determined to fulfil this vow. He would thereby have a safe and easy passage from Europe to Asia, and thus his dominions in the two continents would be securely linked together. He would be free from apprehension as to the approach of an enemy's fleet from the west. As however the spot was but five miles distant from Constantinople, a fortress on it would be a direct menace to the city. It was natural that the emperor should remonstrate. The act could not possibly be reconciled with the sultan's peaceful professions. In his reply to the emperor's ambassadors Mahomet showed very clearly what was in his heart. " Have you the right or the power to contest my actions on my own ground?" It was his ground because, as he went on to say, " as far as the shores of the Bosporus Asia was inhabited by the Turks, and Europe deserted by the Europeans." He regarded it, it would seem, as bought with Turkish money, in consideration of the pension paid to the Ottoman prince, and as therefore Turkish property. " My resolutions," he added, " surpass the wishes of my predecessors." There could no mistake about the meaning of such language. The emperor saw now that he might as well draw the sword at once, and he would have done so, for he was a man of high spirit, but he was persuaded by his craven ministers to look on quietly while his perfidious enemy was surely preparing the means of his ruin.

The sultan was a man whom nothing could turn from a purpose once formed. In the spring of 1452 he began his fortress, for which abundant materials had been transported by a host of zealous labourers from the forests and quarries of the neighbouring regions of Asia Minor. He presided himself over the work, and inspired the vast multitude of workmen with his own enthusiasm. When it was completed it presented a triangle, with a tower at each of the angles. Two of the towers faced the main land, the third and loftiest looked seaward. Their walls, which were covered with lead, were thirty feet in breadth, while the intermediate fortifications were twenty-two feet, and thus it was a fortress of the first class, on which the heaviest artillery then in use could easily be mounted. Mahomet had now an admirable base of operations. While the work was in progress, some trifling acts of hostility had occurred, sufficient, however, thoroughly to alarm the city. The emperor had asked that his subjects in the outlying villages might have the protection of a Turkish military guard, while they were gathering in their harvest, as otherwise they would be at the mercy of the savage and fanatical host which was ransacking the country far and wide for whatever might be of use in the construction of the fortress. The result was a fray between the retinue of an Ottoman chief and some Greek villagers, and blood was shed on both sides. The emperor had the city gates closed, and sent the sultan a final message, in which he declared his resolve to defend his people to the last. The sultan's reply was equally defiant, and in the autumn of 1452 war was in fact begun. A few slight attacks were made on the outworks of the city, with the view of ascertaining and testing its real strength. Having so far acquainted himself with the nature of the work on which he was about to enter, Mahomet, on the first of September, retired to Adrianople. There in good earnest he prepared for the siege, which he meant to begin in the following spring.

Two of the emperor's brothers were then in the Peloponnese, still under Greek control, and were ruling it with the title of "despot." They had a force under their command, which the sultan determined to hold in check, lest it should come to the succour of the city. A numerous army was marched into the country under one of his pashas, and the resistance of the princes, though spirited, was unavailing. From that quarter there was no help for the emperor in his distress. The sultan could forthwith pursue his plans and preparations throughout the winter without fear of interruption. His whole time was passed in taking counsel with his military and engineering officers, and in sounding the temper of his soldiers, among whom he is said to have frequently wandered in disguise. His chief minister, Khalil, saw that it was useless to attempt to turn him from his purpose, and when suddenly summoned into his presence, trembling perhaps under the consciousness that his friendship for the

Greeks made him almost a traitor to his master, replied to the eager sultan, who had asked from him the gift of Constantinople, that "God, who had already given him so much of the Roman empire, would not deny the remnant and the capital."

One of the most remarkable features of the siege of Constantinople was the strange blending which it witnessed of the methods of ancient and modern warfare. It was by this time clearly evident that artillery was destined to play a great part in the wars and sieges of the future. But as yet the discovery was not sufficiently perfected to enable combatants to dispense with those old engines of the Greeks and the Romans, the catapult and the ballista. These were still retained, and were used with effect on the present occasion. Amurath, as we have seen, had however employed a few pieces of ordnance in his assault on the city in 1422. It has ever been the instinct of the Turk to utilise promptly the newest and most efficient instruments of destruction. Mahomet made a special study of artillery, and secured the assistance of foreign genius in rendering this arm more powerful than it had hitherto been made. Neither Turk nor Greek had as yet acquired the art of casting large guns, such as would be serviceable for the purposes of a siege. For this they were obliged to resort to the foreigner. One Urban, a Wallachian, an adept in this new science, had been in the Greek service, but he seems to have been poorly remunerated, and his pay had even fallen into arrears, and so he was now tempted to leave the Greek for the Turk. The sultan was sure to be a good paymaster. "Can a cannon," he asked, "be cast capable of throwing a ball or stone of sufficient size to batter the walls of Constantinople?" On the strength of the engineer's favourable reply, a foundry was established at Adrianople, and a great gun cast, with a mouth exceeding two and a half feet in diameter, and capable of projecting to the distance of about a mile a missile of six hundred pounds weight. Other cannon, it is said, were cast for bullets of a hundred and fifty pounds. Mahomet, we may be certain, provided himself with as effective a train of artillery as the skill of his day was able to create. His great piece of ordnance was dragged from the foundry to its position before the walls of Constantinople on a framework of thirty carriages by sixty oxen, two months being consumed in the journey. By the 6th of April, 1453, the siege had fairly begun.

What the actual strength of Mahomet's force was, when it sat down to the siege, we cannot say with any certainty. Certain it is, however, that it was such as to preclude all reasonable hope of a successful defence in the absence of foreign aid. Amurath's army is said to have numbered two hundred thousand, and Gibbon thinks it probable that Mahomet's may have been quite as numerous. He may well have had in addition to his regular troops a vast swarm of volunteers, attracted by zeal in a holy cause and the hope of boundless plunder. Phranza, who ought to have had some means of knowing, but who, no doubt, might be tempted to exaggerate, speaks of an army of two hundred and fifty-eight thousand, and subsequent writers magnify it into three or four hundred thousand. An incredulous Greek,[1] indeed, has stated that in his belief all the Turkish forces, horse and foot, could not have exceeded eighty thousand, and he describes them as a mere pitiful handful of barbarians. Finlay, we observe, accepts this estimate. It may not be easy to see how Mahomet could possibly have provided for the needs of a much larger army, but we must remember that he was utterly reckless of human life so long as he could attain his ends, and we rather incline to think it possible that he may have entered on the siege with at least a hundred thousand men. He had a numerous, though not by any means a formidable, fleet. It was, in fact, for the most part simply made up of transport vessels and half-decked coasters, which, as the events proved, were no match for Genoese and Venetian galleons. At first he had, it is said, thirty triremes or regular warships and a hundred and thirty other vessels; but by the fifteenth of April, a few days, that is, after the commencement of the siege, his fleet had been largely reinforced, and numbered in all four hundred and twenty vessels of various description. The city was now closely beleaguered both by land and sea. The enemy's entrenched lines extended from the Sea of Marmora to the Golden Horn, while the suburb of Pera or Galata was threatened by another army. Here were congregated the Genoese, who were not only reluctant to spend their blood and their treasure in defence of the city, but who could not even be thoroughly trusted. Far the best of the sultan's troops for such a work as he had in hand were the janissaries. These

[1] Philelphus, quoted by Gibbon.

numbered about twelve thousand, and were drawn up under the sultan's own eye before the gate of St. Romanus, in the centre of the great wall.

This now famous force had already decided more than one doubtful struggle in favour of the Turks, and had bid fair to become "the arch of Ottoman greatness." Its composition was such as to make it as far as possible a pure military caste, which knew nothing but its master's orders, and was wholly free from the ordinary sympathies and sentiments of mankind. The janissary, like the Jesuit, was an isolated being: he was a simple soldier, without a single home tie, devoted heart and soul to the cause in which he was enlisted. Taken in early childhood by conscription from among the offspring of Christian parents captured in war by the Turks, or purchased, it might be, in the slave-market of Constantinople, he was bred and trained a Mahometan for the special service of his masters. It was probably Orchan, the second prince of the House of Othman, who first exacted from the conquered peoples a tribute of children, and thus, as has been said, turned their strength against themselves. The janissaries were invariably supported by the religious orders of Turkey, with whom from their education they were brought into the closest sympathy. Thus they were felt to represent the Turkish people, and to be, in fact, a national guard, always prepared to stand up for the nation's rights, and thoroughly identified with its history and traditions. To their devotion the Ottoman dynasty long owed its stability. In after times, that which had been the empire's strength became its weakness. The janissaries would not hear of the slightest change or reform, and so, when a new military system, adapted to modern warfare, was necessary for Turkey, Sultan Mahmoud, early in the present century, had to clear them out of the way by a *coup de main*. At the time of which we are speaking they had deservedly won a great reputation, and were, in all probability, the best and most highly trained infantry in Europe.

Let us now see what resources the emperor, "the solitary and indigent prince," as Gibbon calls him, had for defence of his ancient and venerable city. One resource, as we have already seen, was conspicuously absent. Of genuine patriotic spirit among the Greeks there was scarce a spark. Rich men would swear they were penniless, rather than contribute to the pay of the mercenaries on whom in their dire extremity they had mainly to depend. In former sieges the luxurious pleasure-loving Byzantine could arm himself and serve on the ramparts, and even endure the miseries of a protracted blockade. But of all this hardly a trace was left. He could repeat prayers and wrangle about the bread in the sacrament and drink confusion to the pope and his satellites in his tavern, but, with the infidel at his gates, he could not shake off the wretched cowardice which he tried to dignify with the name of resignation to the Divine will. The emperor was indeed in a piteous plight. A good and brave man himself, uniting old Roman virtue with Christian faith and fortitude, he would have held his city against the foe, but for the scanty and miserable material with which he had to work. Some of the citizens, both nobles and people of the lower class, had fled from the city before the siege began. The remaining inhabitants would seem to have been for the most part an unwarlike crowd of mechanics, monks, women, and children.

The emperor directed his minister, Phranza, to make diligent search through the city, and to ascertain to the best of his ability how many of the citizens were really able or willing to fight in its defence. The result was deplorable. Phranza, with shame and grief, had to tell Constantine that he could not muster in this great emergency more than four thousand nine hundred and seventy-three volunteers for garrison duty out of the entire population. No more Romans, as Phranza styled these degenerate Greeks, were to be found to defend the city of the Cæsars. To these were to be added about two thousand regular soldiers. Of Greeks there were thus barely seven thousand in arms during the siege. Constantinople, however, was not quite left to its own unaided resources, or the struggle would have very quickly been ended. There was hardly a nation which had any commercial dealings with the city which did not do something, however small, for it in its time of need. Italian volunteers hurried thither, feeling that their own interests were bound up with its safety. Three large galleons and a small body of troops were furnished by the resident magistrate of the Venetians for the special defence of the harbour. The same officer also was charged with guarding the great imperial palace. The consul of the Catalans was likewise among the defenders. Cardinal Isidore, too, a Greek himself by birth, and the metropolitan of Kief, had been sent by Pope Nicholas as his legate in the November of the preceding year, and he also brought with him a small body of troops. But the mainstay of the defence was a brave and noble warrior from Genoa, John Giustiniani, who all his life had been renowned for his daring spirit. Many were the occasions on which he had distinguished himself. Once the king of Aragon, when defeated, had, in admiration of his courage, requested leave to surrender his sword to him in person. Giustiniani came with two large ships and three hundred picked soldiers. John Grant, too, from Germany, an experienced engineer officer, rendered good service. In all, the foreign force in Constantinople numbered about two thousand. Its defence thus rested with a garrison not exceeding nine thousand, yet the emperor had to man a line of wall landwards of five miles in extent, which at every point could be directly assailed by the enemy. Other lines of fortification by the port and on the Sea of Marmora, several miles in length, had to be defended. The task was certainly one beyond human power. Of artillery the emperor is said to have had a hundred and thirty pieces, but these were generally very inferior to the Turkish ordnance. His fleet was good and powerful by comparison, but it was not numerous, consisting only of fourteen ships in addition to the Venetian galleons above mentioned. Of the walls and their capacity for resistance we have already spoken. Their defence was divided and arranged in twelve portions, of which two only were entrusted exclusively to the Greeks. In the remainder the Greeks merely shared the work with the strangers who had come to their aid.

With these very inadequate resources Constantinople had to be held against an army sufficiently numerous at the outset, and doubtless reinforced from time to time by accessions of strength from the Turks in Asia. Mahomet drew his lines, as Amurath, his father, had done, from the harbour to the sea, and erected fourteen batteries at the weakest points of the first of the two landward walls, which, when he had thoroughly battered it, he meant to carry by assault. The most powerful of these batteries were directed against the Charsian Gate and the gate of St. Romanus, and it was at this latter gate that the monster gun was planted. Here, it would seem, the chief assault would be made. Mahomet's lines consisted of earthworks, which screened his men from the enemy's fire, and checked their sorties. He had, indeed, shown from the beginning singular forethought. Among his troops he had some experienced miners, who had been brought from the mines of Novoberda in Servia. He had also a multitude of archers, and his somewhat rude artillery was supplemented, as we have noted, with the battering apparatus of ancient warfare. Not a precaution had been omitted which a great organising genius could devise in order to insure success. Nevertheless, all at first was failure. The great cannon, which could be fired only seven times a day, burst, with a terrible destruction of life. The miners were baffled by the superior skill of the Greek and Latin engineers. The wall, indeed, was here and there broken and shattered, but the great fosse, though again and again filled with fascines and timber and innumerable bodies of slaughtered Turks, so as to afford a passage to the besiegers, was as often cleared by the resolute energy of the garrison under the direction of the emperor and Giustiniani. A wooden portable turret, such as was used in the sieges of antiquity, after having been advanced with much labour during the day against the hostile ramparts, was burnt the following night, and the tower of the gate of St. Romanus, which had been beaten down, was that same night rebuilt, and again defied the fury of the assailant.

Another disaster soon befell the besiegers. It is quite enough to show that the city might even yet have been saved. Four ships, with supplies and military aid, were preparing early in April to sail from Chios to its relief, but were detained in harbour by contrary winds. One bore the Greek, three the Genoese flag. After a while, however, they reached the Bosporus, now wholly blockaded by the Turkish fleet in overwhelming numbers. It might well seem madness to attempt to force a passage. The shores on either side at this critical moment were lined with a multitude of anxious spectators, both Turks and Christians. The hearts of the latter must have sunk within them when they saw the apparent hopelessness of the situation. But the five ships were strong and lofty, and armed with artillery, and handled by men familiar with the sea and with naval warfare. They dashed fearlessly among the frail Turkish craft, pouring out on them their Greek fire, and sinking them with their guns, till the sultan, who had been watching the conflict on horseback from the beach, was beside himself with rage. Twice had the

Turks attacked, and twice been driven off in utter discomfiture, when he shouted at them his angry reproaches, and insisted on a renewal of the conflict. It was all in vain; again his vessels were scattered in disorderly flight, while the brave little relieving squadron rounded the point of St. Demetrius, and entered the harbour in triumph. It seemed, indeed, thus early in their history, as if God had denied to the Turks the empire of the sea, and reserved it for the unbelievers, as they themselves, even in the days of their power, have been ready to confess. Mahomet would have impaled his admiral on the spot, but for the resolute intervention of the janissaries. He had to satisfy his wrath by laying a hundred strokes on the man's back with a ponderous golden rod. The Greeks meanwhile became hopeful, and counted on further and more powerful aid. But nothing more was done for them. It may be that the indifference of Christendom was in some degree due to a superstitious belief said to have been in the air, that the Turkish conquests would end with Constantinople. It admits, however, as we have seen, of another and an adequate explanation.

The sultan, with all his resolution, was seriously discouraged by the discomfiture of his fleet, and had half a mind to relinquish the siege. Fate, it seemed, was against him. The Turks were dismayed by vague rumours of aid said to be advancing from Hungary and from Italy to the rescue of the Greeks. Terror and rage provoked them to say that they had been dragged from their homes to a hopeless enterprise by a despot who would be the ruin of his race. Mahomet's counsellors were depressed and anxious. One of them, Khalil, the chief vizier, we have had occasion to mention. He was at first glad to see the changed temper of his master, and he urged him finally to abandon his design, which, he hinted, would be soon baffled and confounded by a combination of the Western powers. Khalil is said at this time to have been still carrying on a correspondence with the imperial court. This may have been known, or at least suspected, by another minister in the sultan's service, Zagan, a fierce enemy of all Christians, whose steadily warlike counsels in the end prevailed. "Your arms," he is reported to have said to Mahomet, "are far greater than Alexander's ever were. I do not believe in the fleet from Italy which Khalil has said is on the way, nor is there any chance of union among the Western princes, who, from their numbers and clashing interests, cannot agree long together." This was advice much more to the sultan's heart, though for the time he was wavering, than that of the rather timid, if not actually treacherous, Khalil.

Some new mode of attack must, it was clear, be devised. The attempts on the land fortifications had been disastrously repulsed. To penetrate the harbour, defended as it was by a strong chain and several ships, would seem, after the Turks' recent experience of sea fighting, an utter impossibility. It occurred to Mahomet, however, that it might be possible to convey some of his light vessels overland, and launch them in the inner part of the harbour, where, in the smooth and narrow waters they would by force of numbers be more than a match for the enemy's more powerful but far fewer ships. The Venetians, as he would have heard, had lately transported some of their galleys from the river Adige to the lake of Garda; and if he was, as has been supposed, a student of ancient history, his imagination may have been fired by reading of a similar feat which had been accomplished by Augustus after the battle of Actium, and attempted by Hannibal at the siege of Tarentum. The only way in which the sultan's idea could be carried out would be by beginning the work from some point on the Bosporus north of the city. The road would have to be constructed behind the suburb of Pera, occupied by the Genoese. The thing, it was evident, would require the persevering co-operation of a vast multitude, but this Mahomet could command. The space to be traversed was about five miles of hilly wooded ground, and over this a passage for the ships was made, covered with planks that had been carefully greased with the fat of sheep and oxen. The arduous work of transport began, it seems, at Dolma-Baghtché, and ended on the top of the ridge by the cemetery of Pera, and thence down the slope a numerous flotilla was launched in the Golden-Horn. There, in comparatively shallow water, the vessels were safe from attack from the huge Greek galleys, while they threatened the city in a new quarter. But the sultan's work was not yet finished. He had now a fleet and an army in the harbour's innermost recess, where the Greeks were particularly assailable, but it was still necessary to connect his ships with the shore by means of a bridge, on which his men might advance to the assault. The bridge was constructed under the very eyes of the Greeks, and on it was mounted one of the sultan's largest pieces of artillery. We are not to suppose that the garrison quietly allowed all this to be done without any attempt at resistance. But they were far too few in number to resist effectually, and such guns as they had were overpowered by the Turkish fire. In fact, as soon as they had to meet a really formidable assault at a fresh point, their fate was sealed. One desperate effort by night to burn both bridge and ships was made by a gallant band of noble Greek and Italian youths, but it was discovered and frustrated. All were taken and slain. The infamous deed was quickly avenged by the slaughter of two hundred and sixty Turkish prisoners, whose heads were displayed on the walls. The emperor, we should imagine, was the last man to approve in his heart of this horrible retaliation.

The city now had a very dismal prospect before it. The siege had lasted forty days, but it was every day becoming clearer that it could not be sustained much longer. The old walls had at last yielded at many points to the enemy's artillery. The gate of St. Romanus was in ruins, and four of its adjacent towers were demolished. Since the sultan's last success, the line of attack had been greatly extended, far, indeed, beyond the power of resistance yet retained by the small and weary garrison. There was strife between the Genoese and the Venetians, and Giustiniani and the Duke Notaras were at feud, and taunted one another with treachery.

The duke was not a patriot, and though possessed of boundless wealth, would not part with a fraction of it in defence of his country. No wonder that with such an example before them the few rich citizens left in the town hoarded their treasures. The emperor, in sheer desperation, had to resort to an expedient from which his piety must have shrunk. He was forced to pay his troops out of the plunder of the churches, and this was called sacrilege by the wretched monks and ecclesiastics.

Mahomet was now in a position to assault the city with every prospect of success, and for this he made instant preparation on a great scale. He laid all his plans with the utmost care. But first he summoned the emperor for the last time to surrender. Constantine, it is almost needless to say, spurned the overtures he offered, and resolved at all hazards to cling to his capital, though it was abundantly clear that nothing short of an absolute miracle could save it. He had sworn, so he replied to the sultan, to defend the city to the last moment of his life. Mahomet's preparations occupied several days. Meanwhile there was growing terror and discontent and discord among the citizens, which the emperor sought in vain to allay. On the twenty-fourth day of May it was rumoured that the enemy was about to make a grand attack. Very possibly the sultan's vizier, Khalil, gave the emperor intimation of what he might expect. On the twenty-eighth day the Turks were bidden to prepare themselves for the final struggle. Seven times, after their manner, they bathed themselves, fasted, and listened to the exhortations of their dervishes.

The delights of Paradise and the spoil of the city were promised them in the event of victory. They were filled with enthusiasm, and from their widespread camp, which was now one blaze of illumination, rose the well-known Moslem shout, "God is God, and Mahomet is His prophet!"

The Greeks now well knew that the assault was immediately impending. They were in no mood to resist it. "We," says Phranza, "could not help admiring the religious fervour of the Turks; we too fasted and prayed, and carried our sacred images in procession." On the evening of that same day the emperor addressed for the last time the scanty band of warriors which would have to bear the brunt of the terrible attack of the morrow. Phranza puts into his mouth a long and elaborate oration, which of course he never delivered. "I almost doubt," says Gibbon, with his characteristic irony, "whether it was pronounced by Constantine." That he spoke some earnest words of exhortation, and reminded them of the duty which they owed their ancient and illustrious city, we have every reason to believe. This done, he rode to the fortifications, and visited the guards, and inspected every point in the long line of defence. Then he went to the Church of St. Sophia, and there, according to the Latin form, he received his last sacrament. Finally he returned to his palace, took leave of the members of his household, and asked forgiveness for any offence he might have ever given them. And then the last of the Cæsars again mounted his horse and rode forth to the ramparts to meet his fate.

At early dawn on the twenty-ninth of May the Turkish host rushed to the assault, and Constantinople was menaced alike by sea and land. The gate of St. Romanus, the Charsian Gate, and the Blachern quarter, were the points at which the attack was fiercest. The sultan did not spare his men, and his foremost ranks were driven headlong into the fosse and slaughtered wholesale by the fire and missiles of the garrison. It was a sacrifice he could well afford. For two hours the defence was maintained, and it seemed possible that it might be ultimately successful. Above the din and tumult the emperor's voice, it is said, could be heard, urging a final and decisive effort on behalf of the city. Even at this moment we hear of strife between Giustiniani and the Duke Notaras. The latter had the control of the artillery, and for some cause or other he would not grant the urgent request of the Genoese leader for more guns for the defence of the great breach at the gate of St. Romanus. Meanwhile the famous janissaries, who had not yet been engaged, advanced under the sultan's eye to the attack, and the struggle was now at its height. The defence, it is possible, might have been prolonged, but for an unfortunate accident, to which it was usual with the Greeks to attribute the loss of their city. Giustiniani, on whose presence so much depended, was severely wounded in the hand, it would seem (though our narratives on this point vary), and felt himself obliged to quit his post on the ramparts. According to Phranza, the emperor remonstrated with him and implored him to remain, observing that his wound was but slight. His reply was, however, that he would "return by the same way which God had opened for the Turks." Certain it is that the Greeks ascribed this calamity to the cowardice of Giustiniani at this critical moment. The story was that he died in disgrace soon afterwards, a broken-hearted man, in the island of Chios. It is hardly possible for us to arrive at the truth. Gibbon takes the unfavourable view of his conduct which commended itself to Phranza and the Greeks generally, while Finlay maintains that we ought to be slow to charge a man of well-proved courage with pusillanimity. Phranza himself even speaks of him as " hard as adamant." The matter is one which cannot be explained. But had the brave Genoese still stood at his post, he never could have sustained for any length of time an attack made with such overwhelming numbers on the feeble, worn-out garrison. The fight possibly might have been prolonged. As it was, a panic seems quickly to have showed itself as the Turks rushed on with greater fury. A gigantic janissary, Hassan by name, is said to have been the first to climb the ramparts and to lead them to victory. The emperor died, we know, the death of a hero in endeavouring along with a few of his nobles to stem the advancing tide. This is all we know. The exact circumstances of his death are variously reported. His faithful Phranza was in another part of the city, and did not witness his master's end. He represents him as performing prodigies of valour and slaughtering multitudes of the foe with his own hand—like another Samson. His body lay buried under a heap of slain, but the head, says Phranza, was never found, though Mahomet made special inquiry after it. Another account tells us that the sultan sent it as a proof of victory to several of his cities in Asia. The body was ultimately recognised by the imperial golden eagles embroidered on the boots. So fell the last of the Greek emperors, the last, as he may indeed be worthily called, of the Cæsars.

In the panic and flight that followed many were crushed to death in the gate of St. Romanus. Victors and vanquished thronged in a promiscuous crowd into the streets of the city, and another multitude of the enemy had forced the fortifications on the side of the harbour, and had joined themselves to their companions who had just stormed the landward defences. On the twenty-ninth of May, 1453, Constantinople, after a siege of fifty-three days, was in the hands of the infidel. The great calamity which had long been hanging over Christendom was now finally consummated. The poor terror-stricken inhabitants, as soon as they knew the event, flocked for refuge into the Church of St. Sophia, capable, it is said, of receiving twenty thousand people. They barred the doors against the enemy, and encouraged themselves on the strength of a prophecy which declared that when the Turks had penetrated to the space before St. Sophia an angel would descend from heaven, sword in hand, and drive them from the city. Soon the enemy burst into the sacred building and claimed his prey. There was no resistance. Old and young, high-born and low-born, youths and maidens, were hurried away by ruthless hands into captivity, and all parts of the city witnessed like scenes. It is said that sixty thousand Greeks became the conqueror's spoil, and were scattered throughout his dominions. Phranza had to endure slavery for a time, though after a while he was released, and was allowed to ransom his wife; but he had the misery of seeing his children torn from him—his daughter consigned to the sultan's seraglio, and his son, a boy of fourteen, choosing death in preference to dishonour. The great Duke Notaras was the noblest and most distinguished of the prisoners. He showed the sultan, it is said, a vast hidden treasure of jewels and pearls. His fate was a hard one, though he hardly seems to deserve our pity, as it is whispered that he turned traitor after having submitted himself to the victor. At first the sultan flattered him with the hope of safety, but soon afterwards put both him and his two sons to death, thereby in Christian estimation conferring on them the glory of martyrdom. If we are to believe the Greek writers, he was false to his first promises of mercy, and revealed a hideous perfidy in the wholesale massacres which he perpetrated.

Mahomet, it is said, was profoundly impressed with the spectacle of the fallen city. Cruel and perfidious he may have been, but he would allow no wanton destruction, and he reproved with a blow of his scimitar a barbarous Turk whom he saw breaking the marble mosaics in the Church of St. Sophia. In that church, now suddenly converted into a mosque, on its high altar, he offered up his prayers and thanksgivings. In some respects the Turk, after his victory, contrasted favourably with the Latin Crusader. He was more obedient, more amenable to discipline, and his conquest was even accomplished with less bloodshed than that of the Latins, though it undoubtedly consigned the Greek race to greater permanent misery and degradation. The sultan had at least some nobility of character, though it is certain that he stained the glory of his triumphs with some very unworthy deeds. He went from the Church of St. Sophia to the imperial palace, and it was there, as he surveyed the desolate halls, that he is said to have called to mind those pathetic words of a Persian poet: "The spider's curtain hangs before the portal of Cæsar's palace; the owl is the sentinel on the watch-tower of Afrasiab."

The promised plunder could hardly have disappointed the sultan's eager and victorious soldiers. The Turk was certainly not more greedy and rapacious than the Latin conqueror had been. Constantinople, indeed, was very poor compared with what it had been in the days of its greatness. Ever since the Latin conquest its wealth and population had steadily declined. Of the spoil taken by the Turks, far the largest and most valuable portion consisted in the captives themselves. These would be sold into slavery, if they or their friends were unable to save themselves by the payment of a good ransom. There must, however, have been some richly furnished houses, and many private treasures, which the possessors had grudged the emperor, when he wanted money for his troops. The churches, too, and the monasteries must have yielded a handsome booty. We can quite understand how it came to be said of a Turk, who had suddenly grown rich, that he had been at the sack of Constantinople. The Genoese of Galata contrived to save themselves and their most valuable property. While the Turks were intent on the pillage of the city, they sailed out of the harbour and made good their escape.

The sultan had now to undo the work of destruction. Constantinople was henceforth to be the capital of his empire. For this honour "the genius of the place" had clearly marked out the city of Constantine. The character of Ottoman dominion was soon impressed on it, yet at the same time the rites of Christian worship were celebrated in several of its churches, and the patriarch was acknowledged by the sultan, and even received from his hand the crosier which symbolised his sacred office. Many a Greek felt that he could return in safety to the city of his fathers, and he was encouraged by the conqueror to do so. From Roumania and Asia Minor as many as five thousand families were summoned by his order to leave their homes and take up their abode in his new capital. What he could, the sultan certainly seems to have done, for the revival of the prosperity of Constantinople.

The fall of the city had long been expected throughout Europe, and Pope Nicholas V. had, as we have seen, actually prophesied it. It would seem, at least in many quarters, to have been anticipated without any excessive dread or sense of disgrace. Yet, when it actually occurred (though some spoke of it as a *Divine judgment* on persistence in heresy), it appears to have confounded Christendom with shame and horror, and men talked of another Crusade. An old and venerable fabric had been destroyed, and the gap was filled by a barbarous and infidel power, whose very nature and instinct it was to make war upon Christian faith and society. But for good and sufficient reasons the Western princes and their peoples could not be shamed or frightened into a common effort for the deliverance of Europe from the Turk. Nothing was done; nothing was likely to be done; though some feeble and fitful attempts were made soon afterwards by Pope Pius II. Yet that very pontiff, before his elevation, had himself, in a sketch of the state of Europe, spoken strongly of the hopelessness of any such project, and described Christendom as "a body without a head." For us, indeed, it has been in many ways a misfortune that the Turk was allowed to retain his prey, though perhaps it was no less difficult then than now to see who was to take his place, even if it had been practicable to dispossess him. It has undoubtedly left us a legacy of perplexity and confusion. The fall of Constantinople is, indeed, a very dark chapter in the annals of mankind. There is little to relieve the darkness. If the scattering of the city's literary treasures helped on the revival of learning, there was, we know, a woeful destruction of manuscripts, which every scholar must deplore. At this point we take leave of its history, which now becomes that of the Ottoman power in Europe.

RECENTLY PUBLISHED.

LIFE AND ADVENTURES OF ERNST MORITZ ARNDT, the Singer of the German Fatherland. Compiled from the German. Crown 8vo, cloth, 7s. 6d.

ISLAM UNDER THE KHALIFS OF BAGDAD. By R. D. OSBORN, Major in the Bengal Staff Corps. Price 12s. cloth.

"A most valuable contribution to public information on that which is now the leading question of the day."—*English Independent.*

LETTERS FROM EGYPT, to Plain Folks at Home. By MARY L. WHATELY. With Engravings. Crown 8vo, 3s. 6d. cloth.

THE ANCIENT NATION: a Sign and a Wonder. With 21 Illustrations. Price 5s.

"A series of conversations on Jewish history, drawn up with much sense and spirit."—*Guardian.*

"The book is full of information, but its best use will be to promote the study of the Bible."—*Record.*

SWITZERLAND AND THE SWISS. Sketches of the Country and its Famous Men. By the Author of "The Knights of the Frozen Sea," &c. &c. With 24 Illustrations. Crown 8vo, 5s. cloth.

"It is pleasantly written, and will be found entertaining reading."—*John Bull.*

"A readable little volume, pleasantly put together."—*Spectator.*

THE LIFE AND REIGN OF EDWARD I. By the Author of "The Greatest of the Plantagenets." Post 8vo. With Portrait. Price 6s. cloth.

"A masterly and valuable contribution to the literature of English history."—*Spectator.*

"The author stands on a much higher level than most admiring biographers. The book is one of great interest and argumentative power."—*Saturday Review.*

THE GREATEST OF THE PROPHETS: a Life of Moses. By the Author of "Essays on the Church." Post 8vo. With 8 Illustrations. Price 6s. cloth.

"We commend it for the information it contains; but we commend it rather as a striking book, full of shrewd sense, clear statement, and intelligent interpretation of the sacred records."—*Christian Observer.*

HISTORY OF FRANCE. Adapted from the French. For the Use of English Children. By EMMA MARSHALL, Author of "Life's Aftermath," &c. With 26 Illustrations. Price 5s. cloth.

"It is pleasant reading, and gives a vivid idea of French history, without overloading the youthful memory with needless details."—*Saturday Review.*

A CENTURY OF DISCOVERY: an Account of the Spanish and Portuguese Navigators, from Prince Henry to Pizarro. From the German of THEODORE VOGEL. With 12 Illustrations. 5s. cloth.

RECENTLY PUBLISHED.

KING AND COMMONWEALTH: a History of the Great Rebellion. By B. MERTON CORDERY and J. SURTEES PHILPOTTS, M.A., Head Master of Bedford School. Third Thousand. Crown 8vo. With Maps and Plans. Price 5s. cloth.

"Well and clearly written, and gives, in a convenient form, a great deal of interesting information. It will be found suitable, not only for the student, but also for the general reader."—*Saturday Review.*

MODERN FRENCHMEN: Five Biographies. By PHILIP GILBERT HAMERTON, Author of "Round my House," &c.

I. Victor Jacquenot.   III. François Rude.
II. Henry Perreyve.   IV. Jean Jacques Ampére.
V. Henri Regnault.

Post 8vo, price 7s. 6d. cloth.

"Mr. Hamerton may claim the praise of having written a book which it will do everybody good to read."—*Examiner.*

"Mr. Hamerton has succeeded in giving the world a very delightful series of short and simple biographies in these charming pages."—*Standard.*

ROUND MY HOUSE: Notes of Rural Life in France in Peace and War. By PHILIP GILBERT HAMERTON. Third Edition. Cloth 5s.

"Mr. Hamerton has had singularly good opportunities of observation. He has also the powers required in a good observer. He has the eye of a painter, and he is a man of singularly liberal mind."—*Saturday Review.*

COUNTRY LIFE IN SYRIA. Passages of Letters written from Anti-Lebanon. By HARRIET RATTRAY. With 12 Illustrations. Price 3s. 6d. cloth.

"Very interesting notes by a lady who has spent twelve years among the peasantry of Syria. Sketches of life, character, and adventure, &c.

AMONG THE ARABS: ADVENTURES IN THE DESERT, and Sketches of Life and Character in Tent and Town. With numerous Illustrations. Price 3s. 6d.

"A work containing much information, arrayed in a manner likely to suit young readers. It is well suitable for a Christmas present to a boy."—*Standard.*

STORIES FROM HOMER. By the Rev. ALFRED J. CHURCH. With 24 Illustrations after Flaxman, tinted in the style of the Greek vases. Sixth Thousand. 5s. cloth.

Mr. Church has long since proved himself a ripe and good scholar, though he had given evidence of the Homeric insight which this charming volume displays."—*turday Review.*

STORIES FROM VIRGIL. By the Rev. ALFRED J. CHURCH. With 24 Illustrations after Pinelli. Cloth, 5s.

SEELEY, JACKSON, AND HALLIDAY, FLEET STREET, LONDON.

www.ingramcontent.com/pod-product-compliance
Lightning Source LLC
Chambersburg PA
CBHW032113230426
43672CB00009B/1718